Marguerite Pindling
A BIOGRAPHY

Gail Saunders

Macmillan Education
Between Towns Road, Oxford, OX4 3PP
A division of Macmillan Publishers Limited
Companies and representatives throughout the world

www.macmillan-caribbean.com

ISBN: 978-0-230-72265-1 (PB)
ISBN: 978-0-230-40025-2 (HB)

Text © Gail Saunders 2009
Design and illustration © Macmillan Publishers Limited 2009

All rights reserved; no part of this publication may be reproduced, stored in a retrieval system, transmitted in any form or by any means, electronic, mechanical, photocopying, recording, or otherwise, without the prior written permission of the publishers.

The publisher and author wish to thank the following rights holders for the use of copyright material:

Extract from *Bahamian Review*, August 1987, p13 by Basil Smith reprinted by permission of Basil Smith; extract from *Report of the Commission of Inquiry appointed to inquire into the Illegal use of the Bahamas for trans-shipment of Dangerous Drugs destined for the USA November 1983–December 1984*, Nassau Bahamas Government, 1984, pp402–408, public domain; extract from *The Life and Times of Sir Oscar Lynden Pindling, First Prime Minister of the Bahamas*, Macmillan, 2002, p389 and extract from article by Andrew Coakley from *Nassau Guardian*, 3 June 1987, reproduced by permission of the Sir Lynden Pindling Foundation.

If any copyright holders have been omitted, please contact the publishers who will make the necessary arrangements at the first opportunity.

Typeset by EXPO Holdings
Cover design by Mike Brain Graphic Design
Cover photographs by Andrew Toogood (front) and Leeroy Burrows (back)

Printed and bound in Malaysia

2013 2012 2011 2010 2009
10 9 8 7 6 5 4 3 2 1

Contents

	Foreword	iv
	Acknowledgements	vi
	List of Illustrations	vii
1	Early Life	1
2	Move to Nassau – Courtship and Marriage	12
3	A Young Wife – Work, Politics and the Coming of Majority Rule	17
4	Life as First Lady 1967–1980s	29
5	Lady Pindling and the Bahamas Red Cross	43
6	Lady Pindling and Politics I	55
7	Lady Pindling and Politics II	68
8	Memorable Moments in the International Arena	75
9	Two Defeats and Retirement from Politics	83
10	Life after Sir Lynden	89
11	Her Children Speak	98
	Epilogue	116
	Notes	119
	Index	121

Foreword
by Sean McWeeney

From the remote and primitive settlement in South Andros where she was born, to the national and international stages that she has graced for more than half a century with her scintillating wit, elegance and charm, there are few Bahamian stories more compelling than the life-story of Dame Marguerite Pindling.

As wife, best friend, collaborator and confidante to the late Sir Lynden Pindling, Dame Marguerite played perhaps a greater role than any other single individual in securing his rise to the pinnacle of Bahamian politics and his success in nine consecutive parliamentary elections (spanning more than 40 years), six of which would see him appointed Premier or Prime Minister. With her legendary instinct for sniffing out traitors, her decisiveness in exposing the plots and derailing the plans of pretenders to the throne, Dame Marguerite was the original "Iron Lady" of Bahamian politics. She took no nonsense from anybody, least of all from those who, from time to time, sought, by fair means or foul, to wrest the crown from her husband's head.

Dame Marguerite's role in the consolidation of Sir Lynden's political supremacy is a story that until now has not been told. Oral tradition and literature alike have tended to portray Dame Marguerite as a peripheral figure of glitz and glamour whose influence upon her husband and the movement he led was negligible. The truth, however, is decidedly otherwise. Although indeed a lady of spectacular beauty and a fashion plate of iconic stature, Dame Marguerite was, at a deeper level, a politician of exceptional ability and skill. Her influence upon the party membership, especially at grass-roots level, and even more especially among the women of the party – then, as now, the backbone of the PLP – was truly enormous. What perhaps is less understood, however, is that this influence derived as much from Dame Marguerite's own personal magnetism and political adroitness as from her connection to Sir Lynden. She was always a formidable figure. The historical reality, therefore, is that her public persona came to full flower not as an appendage to Sir Lynden but as a political phenomenon in her own right, first within the confines of the party and later on the wider national stage.

Dame Marguerite's life, however, has stretched over a much wider and more diversely textured canvas than politics alone. She has also been an important contributor to the development of charitable activism in The Bahamas, most notably, though by no means exclusively, through her pace-setting involvement with the Bahamas chapter of the International Federation of Red Cross. The story of her energetic and dedicated outreach to the poor and the needy, the disadvantaged and distressed, through her work with, and fund-raising appeals on behalf of, the Red Cross, is here told in full for the first time.

No biography of Dame Marguerite would be complete without a portrayal of her role as wife and mother and an appreciation of the surpassing importance of family in her life. This book does not disappoint here either. What is truly remarkable is just how unwaveringly fixed Dame Marguerite's focus on domestic life remained even while she was attending to her many and varied public duties, especially as First Lady.

Having had the honour and advantage of reading this book in draft, I can predict with confidence that it is destined to become one of the classics of Bahamian historiography. That it has been researched and written by Dr Gail Saunders – herself an important and justly celebrated figure in the modern culture of The Bahamas as the foremost historian of our times – is an assurance that this work is of the highest quality, as indeed it is, made even more so by the judiciously selected photographs that accompany the text. These photographs tell a story of their own because they convey, so much more than mere words ever could, the beauty, poise and charismatic appeal – and some of the important milestones in the journey – of the wonderful lady who is the subject of this important, interesting and long overdue book.

Dame Marguerite can be assured of her place in Bahamian history: as a freedom-fighter and suffragette, as the political partner of the man who is, by common acclaim, the greatest Bahamian of all times, as a patriot par excellence, as the quintessential First Lady, as a charitable worker, and as a devoted wife, mother and grandmother. The many varied threads of Dame Marguerite's life together constitute a dazzling tapestry that will be studied and admired and saluted by successive generations of Bahamians including our own.

Marguerite Pindling is a national treasure. This book explains why.

September 2008

Acknowledgements

I consider it a singular honour to have been asked by Dame Marguerite Pindling to write her biography. She must be thanked for the confidence she placed in me, for her cooperation and patience over the last four years. My thanks to her children, Obi, Leslie, Michelle and Monique for their assistance, and for speaking so candidly about their mother.

Gratitude is owed to all those who were interviewed including the Pindling children, the late Enid Duncombe, Vernice Moultrie Cooper, Sir Arthur Foulkes and A. Leonard Archer.

A huge debt of gratitude is owed to Sean McWeeney for reading the manuscript, for his insightful comments which did much to improve the book and for writing the Foreword.

Special thanks to many persons who contributed to making the book a reality: Helen Smith for her patience and efficiency in typing the manuscript, Ivy Curry for clerical assistance, Jennifer Minnis for editorial assistance, Joanne Maura for research, the Department of Archives and the Red Cross Association for cooperation and for information.

My thanks to historian Michael Craton whose biography: *Pindling: The Life and Times of Lynden Oscar Pindling (1930–2000), First Prime Minister of The Bahamas* was an important source, as was Patricia Beardsley Roker's *The Vision of Sir Lynden Pindling in His Own Words*. I am also grateful to the Broadcasting Corporation of The Bahamas for airing the various programmes about the Pindlings on ZNS TV and Radio.

When I began the book, my husband, Winston Saunders, always encouraged and supported me. His comments on each chapter were most helpful. Regrettably, he did not live to see the finished product. I only hope he would approve. Other members of my family, my father, Basil North, brother, Terry North and his family helped to sustain me over the period in which this book was written.

Gail Saunders, 2008

Photographic acknowledgements

The photographs are from the Pindling family collection, unless stated otherwise. Certain photographers and copyright holders must be thanked, including: Leroy Burrows, Stanley Toogood, Andrew Toogood, Helena Lightbourn, Howard Glass, Roland Rose, William Roberts, Roy Newbold, Peter Ramsey, Derek Smith, Vincent D. Vaughan, Bruce Delancey, June Stevenson, Eddie Deveaux, Franklyn Ferguson, Bahamas Ministry of Tourism, Bahamas Information Services, Bahamas Tourist News Bureau, Estate of Dame Doris Johnson and the Crystal Palace Hotel and Casino.

List of Illustrations

1. Reuben, Viola and Bertie McKenzie (Marguerite's parents and half-brother)
2. The house in which Marguerite McKenzie grew up in Long Bay Cays, Andros
3. The house Marguerite Pindling built for her mother in the early 1960s
4. Marguerite McKenzie on the back porch of her sister's house on Augusta Street, Nassau
5. Marguerite McKenzie on the Market Wharf, Nassau
6. Marguerite McKenzie in her sister's house in Augusta Street, Nassau
7. Marguerite McKenzie at her brother's house in Virginia Street, Nassau
8. Marguerite McKenzie when she worked for Stanley Toogood Studios. *Photo:, Leroy Burrows*
9. Lynden and Marguerite Pindling leaving St Anne's Anglican Church after their wedding
10. The wedding party
11. Lynden Pindling opens the door for his bride
12. Marguerite Pindling – a portrait by photographer Mrs June Stevenson
13. Lynden and Marguerite Pindling on his first day in Parliament
14. Leader of the Opposition Lynden Pindling and Marguerite Pindling at Clifford Park, 1964
15. Mr and Mrs Pindling with their children, Leslie, Obi and Michelle, 1967
16. Lynden and Marguerite Pindling with Cyril Stevenson and June Stevenson. *Photo: Maxwell Stobbs, Maxwell's Studio*
17. Official portrait of Mr and Mrs Pindling, 1968, at their Soldier Road residence
18. Marguerite Pindling in the 1960s. *Photo: Howard Glass, Ministry of Tourism*
19. Marguerite Pindling and Lynden Pindling with Michelle and Obi in the late 1960s. *Photo: William Roberts, Bahamas Ministry of Tourism*
20. Marguerite Pindling with Monique and Michelle and their dog 'Sneeze'. *Photo: Howard Glass, Ministry of Tourism*
21. Mrs Pindling meets Mr and Mrs Roy Hamilton, late 1960s. *Photo: Eddie Deveaux*
22. HM the Queen, HRH the Duke of Edinburgh, Robert Symonette, Mrs Diane Symonette, Lynden Pindling, Leader of the Opposition and Mrs Pindling and Obi Pindling in 1966. *Photo: Ministry of Tourism*
23. Marguerite Pindling with Michelle, Leslie and Obi, early in 1967.
24. Marguerite Pindling casts her vote on 10 January 1967. *Photo courtesy of the Estate of Dame Doris Johnson*
25. Marguerite and Lynden Pindling in Detroit, Michigan, 1962
26. Lynden and Marguerite Pindling return to Nassau, 1967. *Photo courtesy of the Estate of Dame Doris Johnson*
27. Lynden Pindling, HM the Queen and the Duke of Edinburgh and Premier Sir Roland Symonette, 1966. *Photo: Roland Rose, Bahamas Ministry of Tourism*

28. Marguerite Pindling and Obi (her son) on the day of his christening, 1959
29. Marguerite Pindling, Dorrith Stockdale (Grant), Mr Stanley Toogood, Leroy Burrows and Helena Bowe Lightbourn
30. Marguerite Pindling with Leslie, Michelle and Obi in about 1964. *Photo: Leroy Burrows, Toogood Studios*
31. Marguerite Pindling in the gardens of the British Colonial Hotel, 1964. *Photo: Stanley Toogood*
32. Marguerite Pindling with Obi, Michelle and Leslie, 1967. *Photo: Frederick Maura, Bahamas Ministry of Tourism*
33. Lynden and Marguerite Pindling with Monique at her christening. *Photo: Howard Glass, Bahamas Ministry of Tourism*
34. Marguerite Pindling at home with Monique. *Photo: Howard Glass, Bahamas Ministry of Tourism*
35. Marguerite Pindling poses at the side of her portrait. *Photo: Howard Glass, Bahamas Ministry of Tourism*
36. Mrs Cindy Williams presenting her cookery book to Mrs Marguerite Pindling. *Photo: Howard Glass, Bahamas Ministry of Tourism*
37. Shortly after Independence: Sir Leonard Knowles, Sir Milo Butler, Governor-General, Mr Lynden Pindling, Prime Minister; Lady Knowles, Lady Butler, Mrs Marguerite Pindling. *Photo: Bahamas Information Services*
38. The Pindlings attend the opening of the Maura Lumber Company
39. The Pindlings in the 1980s
40. Mrs Joy Williams, chairman of Woman 85, presents a cheque to Lady Pindling
41. Mrs Pindling dancing a ring play dance, late 1970s. *Photo: Bahamas Ministry of Tourism*
42. Marguerite Pindling with actress Rhonda Fleming
43. The Pindlings at the opening of Royal Bank House
44. Mrs Pindling with other Ministers' wives at Marlborough House, London, 1972. Thelma Macmillan, Zoe Maynard, Christine Francis, Lady Butler, Beryl Hanna and Marguerite Pindling *Photo: Howard Glass, Bahamas Information Services*
45. Sidney Poitier's honorary knighthood at Government House. *Photo: Bahamas Information Services*
46. Mr and Mrs Lynden Pindling at their 25th anniversary luncheon, 5 May 1981. *Photo: Toogoods*
47. The Pindlings and their children at the premiere showing of *Buck and the Preacher*. *Photo: Bahamas Tourist News Bureau*
48. Vernice Cooper, Zoe Maynard, Clement Maynard, Michelle Pindling, Marguerite Pindling, Winston Saunders, Gail Saunders and Mel Doty. At the Beaux Arts Ball. *Photo: Bahamas Information Services*
49. The Pindlings with Mr and Mrs Ted Arison at the opening of the Crystal Palace Hotel, Nassau, 1980s. *Photo courtesy of the Crystal Palace Hotel*
50. Mrs Zoe Maynard, Mr Ellison Thompson and Mrs Pindling. *Photo: Bahamas Ministry of Tourism*
51. Mrs Pindling with students on Andros, 1970s. *Photo: Howard Glass, Bahamas Ministry of Tourism*

ix

52. Mrs Pindling hosting a ladies' luncheon, 1970s. *Photo: Bahamas Information Services*
53. Lady Pindling with Bobby Symonette and Lady Symonette.
54. HM the Queen greets Mrs Marguerite Pindling on a visit to Nassau in 1977. *Photo: Bahamas Information Services*
55. Mrs Pindling and Lady Cumming-Bruce in the Straw Market. *Photo: Bahamas Information Services*
56. Mrs Pindling and HRH the Prince of Wales at the Independence Ball, 1973. *Photo: Bahamas Information Services*
57. Mrs Pindling with Sidney Poitier and Joanna Shimkus. *Photo: Howard Glass, Bahamas Information Services*
58. Mrs Pindling with Harry Belafonte. *Photo: Freeport News*
59. Mrs Pindling visits the House of Commons, London
60. Mrs Pindling at the launching of the SS *Freeport*
61. Marguerite Pindling and Father William Thompson greeting Mr Arthur Hanna
62. Mrs Pindling on her way to the House of Assembly
63. Mrs Pindling hosts a ladies' luncheon at a PLP Convention
64. Lady Darling, Dame Doris Johnson and Mrs Pindling in the early 1970s. *Photo: Vincent D. Vaughan*
65. Signing of the Panama Canal Treaty, 1977
66. The Pindlings with Ernest Strachan, Chief of Protocol in the 1970s
67. Mrs Pindling attends a banquet of the Business and Professional Women's Association
68. Mizpah Tertullien, Lynden Pindling, Lady Butler and Sir Milo Butler at a Testimonial Banquet by the Women's Branch of the PLP, February 1977. *Photo: Bruce Delancey*
69. Mrs Pindling examines a gift of a bottle of perfume from the women delegates at a PLP convention. *Photo: Howard Glass, Bahamas News Bureau*
70. The Pindlings at the White House with Pesident Carter, Mrs Carter, Mr Ford and Lady Bird Johnson, 1977
71. Mrs Angie Brookes, Secretary General at the United Nations, meets the Pindlings
72. Mrs Marguerite Pindling and Mrs Charmaine Johnson
73. Mr and Mrs Pindling on the way to the palace to celebrate the Queen's Silver Jubilee in 1977
74. Mrs Marguerite Pindling and Mrs Carlton Francis. *Photo: Frederic Maura, Bahamas News Bureau*
75. The Pindlings at the Family Island Regatta, George Town
76. The Pindlings with Rev. Edwin Taylor and Mrs Taylor.
77. HM Queen Elizabeth the Queen Mother stops in Nassau. *Photo: Toogoods*
78. A rally in 1977 at Clifford Park. *Photo: Frederic Maura, Bahamas News Bureau*
79. The Pindlings' at the Lyford Cay Club in the late 1960s with Mrs Penny Dauphinot and Mr Clarence Dauphinot

80. Mrs Lynden Pindling, Mrs Leslie Shelton and Lady Gray outside the House of Assembly
81. Lady Pindling with Defence Force officers in the early 1980s
82. Marguerite Pindling, Lynden Pindling and Vernice Moultrie Cooper in Staniel Cay, Exuma, 1970s
83. Lady Pindling speaking at the opening of Casurinas, West Bay Street
84. Mrs Pindling and Lady Cumming-Bruce inspecting the Girl Guides in Mathew Town, Inagua
85. The Pindlings with Mr and Mrs Edward Seaga at CHOGM, 1975, in Jamaica
86. Sir Milo Butler, Governor-General, HM the Queen, Mr Lynden Pindling, Lady Butler, HRH Prince Philip and Mrs Pindling, about 1977
87. Marguerite Pindling, L. B. Johnson, Lynden Pindling and the Hon. Paul Adderley, Minister of Foreign Affairs, at the United Nations in July 1973
88. The Pindlings with Prince Charles during Independence celebrations
89. Sir Lynden and Lady Pindling with Jamaican President Edward Seaga, 1973
90. Mohammed Ali, his wife and friends visit the Pindlings. *Photo: Howard Glass*
91. The Prime Minister and Lady Pindling with Catholic Archbishop Lawrence Burke and Sir Kendal and Lady Isaacs.
92. Mrs Marguerite Pindling dancing with Winston V. Saunders
93. Mrs Pindling – a portrait by Vincent D. Vaughan, 1980
94. Obi Pindling's Call to the Bar, Supreme Court, Nassau, 1980
95. Mrs Pindling with the Red Cross Youth Group at the Red Cross Fair, Government House Grounds
96. Mrs Pindling drawing a raffle ticket for the Crippled Children's Fund. *Photo: Wendell Cleare, Bahamas Tourist News Bureau*
97. Mrs Pindling at the Stapledon School for the Mentally Retarded
98. Mrs Pindling attends the opening of the Garden Clubs of Nassau. *Photo: Lorenzo Lockhart, Bahamas Tourist News Bureau*
99. Mr Billy Dee Williams and Mrs Marguerite Pindling at the official opening of a Red Cross Fair. *Photo: Vincent D. Vaughan*
100. Mrs Pindling with committee members of the Red Cross Fair Committee in Freeport, Grand Bahama, mid-1970s
101. Members of the Red Cross Raffle Committee. *Photo: Andrew Aitken Photography*
102. Mrs Pindling with children from Red Bay, Andros. *Photo: E. Bruce Delancey.*
103. Burning of the Mortgage, Children's Emergency Hostel. *Photo: E. Bruce Delancey.*
104. Mrs Pindling in the garden of the Children's Emergency Hostel,1974. *Photo: Howard Glass.*
105. The Red Cross Fair committee visits Spanish Wells.
106. Mrs Pindling sells raffle tickets for the Bahamas Association for the Mentally Retarded. *Photo: Vincent D. Vaughan*
107. Mrs Pindling making cash donations to various charities
108. Mrs Pindling gives a speech at a PLP women's luncheon, late 1970s. *Photo: Raymond A. Bethel*

xi

109. Lady Pindling speaking at a pre-election fellowship luncheon on 26 July 1992
110. Mr and Mrs Lynden Pindling on the way to the House of Assembly, 1980s
111. The Pindlings being presented to HM the Queen on an official visit, 1993
112. Lady Pindling with Canadian Prime Minister, Brian Mulroney and Mrs Mulroney. CHOGM, Nassau, 1985.
113. The Pindlings with the Prime Minister of Lesotho
114. The Pindlings with the Prime Minister of the Maldives and his wife
115. The Pindlings chat with Mr and Mrs Edward Seaga
116. Guests including Roman Catholic Bishop Burke, Joyce and Telford Georges, Robert Mugabe, President of Zimbabwe, and Sally Mugabe
117. Sir Lynden greets Rajiv Ghandi and Mrs Ghandi
118. HM Queen Elizabeth II greets Lady Pindling, CHOGM, Nassau, 1985
119. Lady Pindling and Sir Lynden with Sir John and Lady Compton of St Lucia
120. Lady Pindling, Sir Lynden and Kenneth Kaunda, President of Zambia
121. Lady Pindling arrives at Government House, Nassau, to dine with HM Queen Elizabeth II, 1993
122. Governor-General Sir Gerald Cash, Lady Cash, HRH Prince Charles, Princess Diana, Lady Pindling and Sir Lynden at Government House, Nassau, 1982
123. Lady Pindling and Sir Lynden at CHOGM, Nassau, 1985
124. Lady Pindling, Sir Gerald Cash, HM Queen Elizabeth II, Sir Lynden and Lady Cash on the Royal Yacht Britannia; CHOGM, Nassau, 1985
125. Mrs Arnold Smith, wife of the secretary to CHOGM, Mrs Julius Nyerere and Mrs Lynden Pindling in October 1973
126. The Pindlings, Prime Minister Hubert Ingraham, Lady Darling and Sir Clifford Darling and Nelson Mandela at Government House, March 1993. *Photo: Franklyn G. Ferguson*
127. Nelson Mandela visits the Pindlings, 1993
128. Mr Lynden and Mrs Marguerite Pindling before attending a dinner at Buckingham Palace
129. The Pindlings at the Royal Wedding, 1981
130. Lady Pindling and Prime Minister Margaret Thatcher at CHOGM, Nassau, 1985
131. Sir Lynden, Mrs Viola Pindling (his mother), Lady Pindling and Arnold Pindling (his father) after Sir Lynden received his knighthood in June 1983
132. Lady Pindling with the wives of Heads of Government in Harare, Zimbabwe, 1991
133. Lady Pindling being presented to HM the Queen at CHOGM, 1985
134. Sir Lynden and Lady Pindling entertain Mrs Rosa Parks at their home
135. Mrs Marguerite Pindling and others attend a service conducted by Rev. Dr Billy Graham
136. Rev. Billy Graham speaking at the Templeton Prize Ceremony in 1982 at Guildhall, London, England. Lady Pindling is second from right.
137. Sir John Templeton, Mrs Pindling, Rev. Billy Graham and H. E. Anthony Roberts, High Commissioner, at Claridge's Hotel, London, early 1980

138. Mrs Pindling with television personality Ephraim Zembalist Jr.
139. Lady Pindling and HRH the Duke of Edinburgh aboard the Royal Yacht *Britannia*
140. The Pindlings on board the Royal Yacht *Britannia*
141. President Gowan of Nigeria, Mr Lynden Pindling, Mrs Victoria Gowan and Mrs Pindling, 1975
142. Sir Clifford Darling, HM the Queen and Lady Pindling at the Commonwealth Heads of Government Meeting in Nassau, October 1985
143. Mrs Pindling with the wife of the Guyanese Ambassador to Great Britain. *Photo: Howard Glass, Bahamas Information Services*
144. Lady Pindling with the Queen of Swaziland at CHOGM in Harare, Zimbabwe, 1991
145. Lady Pindling with Mrs A. N. R. Robinson, Prime Minister of Trinidad and Tobago, at CHOGM in Harare, Zimbabwe, 1991
146. 1980 Templeton Prize Award, Buckingham Palace, London
147. 1980 Templeton Prize Award
148. The Pindlings with the Prime Minister of Canada, Pierre Trudeau
149. General Gowan and Mrs Gowan pay a visit to The Bahamas after CHOGM in Jamaica, 1975
150. Lady Pindling and Sir Lynden Pindling with granddaughter Danielle Johnson, daughter of Monique and Daniel Johnson, at Danielle's christening at St Agnes Parish Church, 1999
151. Sir Lynden and Lady Pindling on New Year's Eve, 1999 at the home of Mr and Mrs Franklyn Wilson
152. Dame Marguerite is sworn in as Deputy to the Governor-General by Sir Burton Hall, October 2006
153. Dame Marguerite Pindling swears in Mrs Cheryl Albury as Justice to the Supreme Court
154. Dame Marguerite Pindling receives cookies from the Girl Guides
155. Sir Lynden and Lady Pindling on a cruise to the Mediterranean in 1999
156. Sir Lynden and Lady Pindling with Anglican Archdeacon William Thompson
157. Pastors lay hands on Sir Lynden when he returns from Johns Hopkins Hospital in Baltimore
158. Dame Marguerite Pindling with His Excellency Abdullah Ahmed Mohamed A-Murad, Ambassador-Designate of the State of Kuwait and his wife
159. Lady Pindling with Gail and Winston Saunders, Professor Rex Nettleford and Ms Minna Israel outside the Dundas Centre for the Performing Arts, about 2004
160. Lady Pindling in the audience at the graduation ceremony at the University of the West Indies
161. The Pindling family on Sir Lynden's 70th birthday, 22 March 2000.
162. Lady Pindling with Dame Ivy Dumont and Sir Orville Turnquest attend the swearing-in of the Honourable Arthur D. Hanna as Governor-General at Government House in 2004

163. Dame Marguerite's Investiture at Buckingham Palace, 21 March, 2006
164. Dame Marguerite outside Buckingham Palace with her insignia, 21 March 2006
165. Dame Marguerite with Sir Baltron Bethel and Obi Pindling at a luncheon after her Investiture at Buckingham Palace
166. Dame Marguerite shows off her insignia with Obi, Leslie and Michelle outside Buckingham Palace.
167. Dame Marguerite presents a wreath at Sir Lynden's mausoleum on 10 January 2008
168. Lady Pindling with members of her committee to assist hurricane victims, 1994
169. Lady Pindling and her granddaughter Holly
170. Dame Marguerite with Evangelist Jacqueline Rahming and Dame Ivy Dumont
171. Dame Marguerite, Michelle Pindling-Sands and the Hon. Perry Christie (then Prime Minister), present Mr Arthur Hanna with the Lynden Pindling Award for Excellence, 2006
172. Presentations by Dame Marguerite and Michelle Pindling-Sands of the Lynden Pindling Award for Excellence
173. Presentation of the Lynden Pindling Award for Excellence to Mrs Nancy Kelly, 2008
174. Presentation of the Lynden Pindling Award for Excellence to Mr Fred Hazelwood, 2008
175. Presentation of the Lynden Pindling Award for Excellence to Mr Henry Storr
176. Lady Pindling, Prime Minister Perry Christie and Dame Ivy Dumont attend the funeral of the late Edward St George, Freeport, Grand Bahama
177. Dame Marguerite congratulates Justice Rubie Nottage after she was sworn in as a Justice of the Supreme Court, 28 April 2008
178. Lady Pindling presents Sir Lynden's biography to Mr Bill Clinton
179. Dame Marguerite with Leslie, Michelle, Monique and Obi
180. Dame Marguerite's grandchildren Lauren and Holly Sands, Danielle and Grace Johnson and Andrew and Lynden Pindling

1
Early Life

An Andros upbringing

Marguerite Pindling is proud of her Andros roots. She often states: "I'm just a barefoot girl from Andros. You don't know how proud I am of my roots." She was born to Reuben Daniel McKenzie and Viola "Mirmie" Duncombe McKenzie on 26 June 1932 at Long Bay Cays, South Andros. She was the fourth of eleven children, three of whom died as infants.

Her father, Reuben Daniel McKenzie, was of Scottish descent, probably a descendant of Joseph McKenzie, an American Loyalist who had received a generous grant of 200 acres in Great Exuma in 1792.[1]

Reuben McKenzie was born in Exuma at Jolly Hall, a village near to the main settlement of George Town. His first marriage was to a black Exumian woman who bore him seven children. The McKenzie family, which was white, was unhappy with his choice of bride (mostly because of her colour) and Dame Marguerite believes that is why he was sent to Andros to manage the coconut orchard owned by the Albert Smith family of Exuma.

After Reuben McKenzie's first wife died, he met and married Viola Duncombe who was affectionately known as "Mirmie". Viola Duncombe was born in High Rock, South Andros to Thomas Duncombe and Margaret Miller Kemp, who later lived in Fort Myers, Florida. Dame Marguerite says that she never knew her grandmother. According to her half-aunt, Ms Enid Duncombe, "Mirmie" as a child lived with her Aunt Alicia Duncombe in Mason's Addition and later was sent back to Andros where she met Reuben McKenzie.

They were married when she was 15 or 16, by Reverend Enoch Backford, Sr in a house on the corner of Mason's Addition off East Street. Soon afterwards they returned to Driggs Hill in South Andros where they raised their large family, including Marguerite Pindling.

Marguerite Pindling did not know her father's parents or his sisters, Julia McKenzie Glass and Adeline McKenzie Smith. The latter was the grandmother of David Elliott Smith who stars in the television series *JAG*. Julia McKenzie married Levi Glass and had several children, including the popular and ever jovial Helen Glass. Levi Glass worked as the caretaker at Salt Cay for the McCutcheon family from Chicago. Dame Marguerite is also first cousin to Marge Scott, mother of Father Peter Scott and attorney-at-law Michael Scott, and second cousin to Howard Glass, professional photographer.

Andros, where Reuben and Viola McKenzie made their home, is the largest island in the Bahamian archipelago, the least important of an insignificant group of colonies. It was one of the poorest parts of the British Empire. In the 1930s, Andros was second to New Providence in terms of population but not of development. It suffered from poverty, underdevelopment and isolation. Travelling between settlements was difficult due to the lack of paved roads. Boats were the means of transportation but this could be difficult because of uncertain weather conditions and an "inhospitable coast".

Sponging was the leading industry in Andros, occupying most of the able-bodied men and boys from 14 years up. Sponges were plentiful in the "Mud" on the west side of Andros. Agricultural pursuits were second to sponging. Leading crops included Indian and guinea corn, sweet potatoes, cassava, peas, beans, onions and other vegetables. Citrus was grown and coconuts were extensively cultivated in the white sand. Commissioner Herman Pyfrom commented in his 1937 Annual Report for the Mangrove Cay District that there was "good available land" to be found at Long Bay Cays, Kemp's Bay and Pleasant Bay.

Reuben McKenzie found it difficult to survive on the meagre wages he was paid as manager of the coconut orchard, so he turned to farming and fishing to support his growing family. He had two farms, one fairly close to home in Millers Coppice, but the other four miles from the homestead in Long Bay (a settlement within Long Bay Cays). At one of his farms, at Yellow Wood Coppice, he grew pineapples. His subsistence crops included cassava, sweet potatoes, peas, corn, onions and sugar cane. It was there that wood was gathered and taken to the family home. Even when it was wet, it gave off a flame and a lovely aroma.

Life was hard and conditions were very basic. The family home, which Marguerite Pindling remembers as "the biggest in the world", had a thatched roof and only two rooms, which were partitioned off with lumber. Her parents slept in grass beds with iron frames. Dried grass was stuffed into flour bags stitched together and although a bit hard, they served as mattresses. The kitchen was in an outside building and had a fire hearth with pots cooking on three rocks. There was also a corn mill and a grindstone. As in most of the Out Island Bahamas, there was an outhouse. Marguerite had a special place where she said her prayers. While on a trip, her father had sent a pair of shoes for her older sister Doris. Alas, they were too small. Marguerite prayed for her father to send them back for her. Miraculously, her prayers were answered. A new pair arrived for Doris and the original for her.

Later on Reuben McKenzie opened a shop in his house. Philip Brown, brother of Lester and Frederick Brown, was the supplier. There was no electricity or running water. Kerosene lamps sufficed: "Ours was bought from 'Ung' Buddy McKinney's shop in Smith Coppice." A well, under almond trees, often with tadpoles, was the water supply. Running water did not come to South Andros until 1968 when Lady Pindling's mother turned the running-water tap on in Congo Town. A wooden tub which previously held salt beef was used as a bath tub until later, when "we moved up in life and my father bought tin tubs". Water had to be drawn at the well for baths, which were taken outside the house. Siblings took turns. When it rained heavily ponds filled and the children swam and washed in the pond. Clothes were also laundered there by rubbing Octagon soap on them: "If it rained heavily tonight the next morning you would hear the people beating the clothes all over the neighbourhood because the water was nice and soft."

Mosquitoes were a nuisance, especially on a calm night. A fire built outside the house using coconut bark was lit to try to get rid of the pests. Sometimes mosquitoes got into the house and smoke was allowed to blow through while coconut fronds were used to brush down the walls.

As in many Out Island settlements, a popular form of leisure was the telling of "Ole" stories, usually in the evening, especially in the moonlight. Children would gather around the adults who would begin the tales with "Once upon a time, was a very good time. Monkey chew tobacco and spit white lime." Dame Marguerite remembers being told the B'Booky and B'Rabby stories, favourites in many West Indian islands. The characters were popularized by Joel Chandler. Stories usually ended "E, Bo Ben, my story end."

Androsians, like most people, were superstitious. Some believed in and practised obeah, a combination of superstition, medicine and worship. Marguerite Pindling heard about obeah but never witnessed it. She did observe, however, that if her mother had a bad dream, she threw salt in the fire before she talked about it. Dame Marguerite does this to this day. When Mrs McKenzie combed her hair, she removed the residue from her comb, rolled it over in the palm of her hands, blew her breath on it and put it under a rock. It was protection against a possible "fix".

Marguerite Pindling remembers a story of a "Jack Malantern", a mythical figure who would walk at night on the beach at Munnings Point. She admits that she never saw him. She was not aware of Chicharnies, which were angered by the cutting down of the forest and were believed to have been responsible for the failure of Neville Chamberlain's sisal plantation near Mastic Point in North Andros.

Everyone awakened early as there were morning chores to complete before school started. Goats were taken out to the Salina, the flat land where jumbey grew, and were tied under the pinecord tree. Wood had to be gathered for cooking the evening meal. Peas were picked after school, put in crocus sacks which were put in the sun and then taken to the house where Marguerite and her siblings shelled them.

Corn was also gathered. Marguerite McKenzie's job on Friday afternoon was to grind a hopper (a large funnel) of corn for the week and she describes how corn was processed:

First you had to crack the corn, then it had to be reground several times before you got the finished product. We had to fan and riddle the grits and get the husk off. Then sift it for flour. I learnt to do all that ... The corn was cracked and ground into a basket. After the first procedure it was emptied into the hopper and it became less strenuous to grind. After it was ground four times, it became lighter and after checking the consistency we emptied it into a fanner.

Then we would riddle the grits from the corn and kept riddling until the heavy husks were off. Sifting was next. The ground corn was sifted into a fanner. Now there was less grits and more flour. This was emptied into another fanner and sifted again. The second lot of flour was combined with that in the first fanner.

The corn meal was used to make gruel for babies. The rest of the meal was combined with white flour and made into bread after adding sugar. The rest of the grits (coarse and fine), was also used. The finer grits was cooked with peas and coconut milk for the evening meal. Coarse grits was cooked in water and raw coconut was grated and squeezed through a sea fan and the milk from the coconut used over the grits as a breakfast dish.

Women and children plaited using coconut straw and white pond top. Marguerite was taught by her mother. The plaiting was done after school, at nights and on Saturdays. The McKenzie girls walked to another settlement to plait with the other girls. Sometimes white straw plait strings were held over the lampshade to blacken the strings, and when the white was used with the brown straw it produced what was known as peas and rice. The girls would often plait some 20 to 25 yards "measured from the nose to finger tips" and then roll it from finger tips around the elbow, pressing with a bottle or cold iron to smooth the rough edges. Rolls of plait were sent with relatives to Nassau where they were sold, and a Mr Damianos used to visit Long Bay Cays to buy the plait. Money earned was used to buy school supplies or even shoes for the McKenzie children.

Food was simple, comprising red corn grits, peas and grits, or just raw coconut milk and grits. There was also Johnny cake with coconut eaten plain, as butter was scarce. Sometimes the bread was dumb (no baking powder was available), "as I like it to this day". There was very little meat or relish. A few chickens and goats were raised, chickens being reserved for Sunday dinner. Occasionally, hog meat was also cooked. When a goat was killed, it had to be corned and dried to cure it as there was no refrigeration available. Fish, conch and lobster were also sometimes available. Fish and conchs were also dried and corned and hung out on the line near the kitchen in the fresh air to dry. Sometimes the buzzards picked them off the line.

Crabs were always an important part of the diet. Andros people appear to Nassauvians to be quite tall and strong and Dame Marguerite attributes this to the diet (coconut, crabs and fish) and the fact that they walked long distances. She describes crabbing and coco plum gathering as a child:

> *In school we would plan to go out five miles in the settlement in the Pine Yard. As we were nearing the Pine Yard we could smell the scent of the pine – a scent I still remember. This is where boat builders used to go and cut masts for their boats. In the Pine Yard were coco plum trees – the white coco plum – and it was like a pond and there were white crabs. We used to catch them in the mangroves. People go there to this day because around this time, the crabs are very fat now and we used to arrange with the school children from the Motion Town area to Smith Coppice and Miller's Coppice where I lived, and we would wake up early and leave around 5 o'clock in the morning to make the long trek in the cool of the morning. You had to catch these crabs running as they would run to the mangrove between the long roots of the trees. I was very smart. I came home with 12 one time, complete with biters, you know. My father never approved of us going. My mother would say, "Oh, let the children go!"*

Marguerite Pindling states that while catching crabs, they used to go through "saw" grass which left you with long scratches, sliced finger tips and cuts that caused discomfort. "The crabs had to be clipped. We brought the day's catch on our heads, or in bags slung over our shoulders. Some were cooked immediately and the rest left on their backs. They sometimes lasted for days."

Viola McKenzie would open the crabs to separate the fat from the back, then clean the bodies and cook them in the grits with coconut milk. She also made fresh leaven bread and if in a good mood, she would make potato or cassava bread. "She also prepared turtle meat for my father when it was available." Mr McKenzie raised a lot of corn, and residents from The Bluff would exchange their crabs for corn and sometimes turtle meat. Marguerite McKenzie found the pungent smell of turtle meat unpleasant and she admits that she has never liked turtle, even to this day.

Like other Caribbean people, Androsians, including the McKenzies, used the West Indian practice of herbal or "bush" medicine. It was particularly popular on the Out Islands as there were no doctors. Marguerite Pindling remembers taking catnip and bay geranium for worms and chewing crab bush for a pain in the stomach. Sometimes Dr Foulkes, father of Sir Arthur Foulkes, former Cabinet Officer, Bahamas High Commissioner to London, and now Director of Bahamas Information Services and Deputy to the Governor-General, used to visit and would tend to the elderly in the community.

Marguerite Pindling and her siblings attended the one-room, all-age concrete school about a quarter of a mile from the settlement of Motion Town. The room was large and open with push-out shutters – not partitioned off. On the wall was a motto:

> **Life is like a grindstone. It either builds you up or grinds you down. It depends on the stuff you're made of.**

School was headed by a Mr Jupiter, a Guyanese. There he taught the 3 Rs – reading, writing and arithmetic – and some geography. Lady Pindling remembers the West Indian and Royal Readers. There were several blackboards with chalk to write with, and easels. Times tables were sung: "Twice 1 are 2. Twice 2 are 4" – right down to 12 times tables.

Most of the 60 or so children who attended the school were poorly dressed and were barefoot. They walked miles from Driggs Hill, The Bluff, Long Bay, Congo Town, High Rock, Duncombe Coppice, Miller's Coppice, Smith Coppice and Motion Town.

The headmaster, Mr Jupiter, was succeeded by Mr H. A. Varence, a Cat Islander, who came along with his wife Charlotte and one son, Winston. "He had a horse named McArthur – we were very afraid of him."

Marguerite McKenzie and her siblings, about three-quarters of a mile away, were slightly more fortunate, possessing books, pencils and slates. They performed fairly well and Marguerite at the age of 12 or 13 became a monitor, being paid a meagre but welcome sum of seven shillings and six pence a month. Her whole salary was spent on "sweet milk" (condensed milk). Children willingly scrubbed the school floor with soap bush or almond leaves and cleaned the yard around the teacher's residence. "The children also kept the headmaster's onion garden by toting seaweed from the beach to fertilize it and covering it with sand. Mrs Charlotte Varence used to visit our school every Thursday to teach sewing. We learnt hem stitching and buttonholing."

Events and cultural happenings

In the 1930s the Mail Boat, a motor vessel called *The Gary Roberts*, owned by a prominent merchant, Sir George Roberts, connected New Providence and Andros. It came every two weeks. The 'Mail' was chartered by the Government to carry the post, but it carried much more than correspondence and parcels. Its decks were usually packed with all sorts of produce: sheep, pigs, fowls, barrels of sisal and sponge as well as people.[2]

Certain food items, like butter, were scarce. The Mail Boat was therefore welcomed with excitement every two weeks into Andros. It would sail from Nassau to Morgan's Bluff in the north down to Drigg's Hill to Mars Bay in the south. It travelled very slowly and by the time it reached Long Bay Cays, the Maple Leaf butter had melted.

The coming of the Mail Boat, as in the lives of most Out Islanders, was an exciting event for Androsians. Everyone came out to greet the boat on Sunday afternoon. "You could hear them shouting, 'The Mail Boat coming.' Then we would run out of Sunday School and dash down the road to meet it." On its arrival at the settlement (Smith Coppice) just opposite the Commissioner's office and post office upstairs and jail downstairs, passengers usually disembarked into a small boat with an outboard motor which conveyed them to the shore, then waded through the water; some women would lift their dresses if the water was too deep. If the tide was too low to accommodate the boat, passengers were carried for the last part of the journey on the back or in the arms of a local man. When Reuben McKenzie rolled up his trousers once to assist passengers, someone made the comment: "Oh damn, McKenzie white." Everyone pitched in to unload the boat and carry items to the shore. It was fun time for children. Some of the boys went swimming – naked of course. People picked out their packages and stood around the Commissioner's office where the mail bag had been set, waiting to hear if their names would be called. "I remember we used to run home with Papa's letters from his sisters in Exuma; he would read them to us."

Andros, like most Out Island communities, had special celebrations at Christmas, but not on the same scale as in Nassau. Dame Marguerite recalls:

It was fun time for us. Then Christmas morning Junkanoo would come. If the wind was blowing from the north, you were able to hear drums coming. Costumes for Junkanoo were old clothes (rags), and brown paper because we didn't have newspaper ... I remember as plain as day. I could hear the drums coming down the road with singing "watermelon spoiling on the vine"... we children would run and hide ... About six or seven fellows came from the neighbouring settlement (men not women). Just drums, saws and rocks in cans ... The Junkanoos never came to the house, we were a little way from the main road. We would stand in the yard and watch them.

Another event to which Marguerite and her siblings looked forward was the concert or programme on Sunday evening at the school house in Motion Town. As in many Out Island settlements, the concert or programme included "dialogues, recitations, addresses, songs and instrumental music before large and usually attentive audiences".[3]

Dame Marguerite remembers her own participation. She recited and sang. "I can remember 'Beulah Land. Sweet Beulah Land' from the Baptist Hymnal. If you pleased the crowd, they would reward you with money pinned on your dress – four shillings, ten shillings or a pound. While you performed, they would pin the note on you and say 'You're good, go back, sing again.'"

She recalls practising for a play. Her oldest sister Louise was also in the play and they sang "Day is dying in the West". "I can hear it right now in that big school house ... It was a fun time for us and everybody from the settlement would come."

Another event, held annually, was Empire Day. No public official such as the Governor or his representative attended, as Andros was isolated and suffered from the lack of proper roads. Nevertheless, the resident population celebrated by holding dances and the plaiting of the maypole under the coconut trees near the beach.

The event of death was of general community interest. It was central to the Afro-Bahamian mentality. As in most of the Bahamian Out Islands, wakes and "setting-up" meetings were held over the dead. In Long Bay Cays, the wake or setting-up was held while the coffin was being built at the Society Hall. Refreshments of coffee, Johnny cake or leaven bread were served. Often there was a secret supply of alcoholic beverages for the men.

The McKenzies were Anglican, attending St Barnabas Church in Smith Coppice at 10 a.m. Sunday school was at 3 p.m. Usually services were conducted by the catechist, Stephen Davis. The priest was stationed at Mangrove Cay (the seat of the Commissioner) as were the servers and acolytes. Dame Marguerite remembers a Father Beste, an American, who was stationed in South Andros, coming to conduct services at St Barnabas.

After church on Sundays the McKenzie family had a visitor, a Mr Knowles. Dame Marguerite remembers:

> *He would come to the house every Sunday and we wanted to have lunch ... my mother prepared enough for her family, she would kill a chicken. We only cooked rice on a Sunday and also chicken or goat mutton and we didn't have enough to offer, only enough for the family, and man that fellow would not leave. He would sit there and sit there and he would even go to sleep in a chair by the door in the corner and we were getting hungrier and hungrier. So us children would turn the broom upside down in the corner and put salt in the broom or we would go in the dilly tree and shout "the Mail coming". Once you said the Mail coming he would leave. Mama would serve lunch. Papa would grace the table. Then we would go and get something to eat and by that time the rice was cold and hard in the pot. But it was fun.*

Later in the afternoon the McKenzie children attended Sunday school.

For recreation, Marguerite McKenzie and her siblings played the usual children's games. She remembers participating in Ring Play. On Sunday afternoons after Sunday School they enjoyed rounders on the beach. Dame Marguerite also states: "I loved to shoot marbles. I used to shoot marbles with the boys in the yard" – in spite of her father's disapproval. She also made tops and spun them. "We used to play peggin the tops." Another popular pastime was skipping. She recalls: "We used to skip with rope made from bay hop, a long vine with purple flowers that grows on the beach."

Swimming was also popular. Marguerite McKenzie learnt to swim through necessity. "I was forced to learn to swim, for the fellows would throw you in the water and make you learn how to swim."

The McKenzie children used to visit their half-brother Bertie in Drigg's Hill and their great-grandmother in High Rock, usually on Saturdays. Bertie McKenzie, a carpenter, fisherman, farmer, sent fish, conch and lobsters (called "relish") for the week to Reuben and Viola. "My brother George and myself had to walk the five miles on sandy road, or the beach if tide was low, to bring the fish home."

Dances were held in the school house where older people danced the quadrille and the "kapolka" (heel and toe polka). Reuben McKenzie did not allow Marguerite or her siblings to attend. He provided his own entertainment at home, being quite a serious musician himself. He possessed an accordion which he played quite well and also sang songs such as "My Bonny Lies Over The Ocean", "O Please Meet Me Tonight in the Moonlight" and "O Liza See Me Here".

> *Yes, he played that for us but he never played publicly, only privately at home to entertain the family. He was not a flamboyant person; he was always so very serious, as a matter of fact we were more afraid of him than anything. I remember he whipped me once for stealing peanuts. Those were the peanut seeds he had picked out for planting. He kept them on a shelf and you had to climb up. I climbed up and couldn't get down because he was standing there looking at me. "What are you doing?" And I could not remember what I said; he took off his belt and he gave me a few whacks and said: "Don't ever steal from your parents, you must always remember, if you want something, you ask for it." That was the first and last time he ever whipped me. My mother was the one who was the disciplinarian. Mama! Oh yes. You had to get your own switch. My father used his belt but my mother used to send us for our own switch. If it was small you had to go back and bring a bigger one. She used a tamarind switch more than anything else because it was right by the kitchen door, so you had to go and get it. I am sure that all parents were the same. If you did something and they didn't whip you for it then, they would store that up until you did something worth a licking, and my mother would whip every one of us. You come here – you get yours too for whatever we might have done. You had to cry "Oh Mama don't beat me." But you know, it didn't kill us. It made us children better adults. When we, the sisters, get together here at home, especially at Christmas time, when we have our family meal and we talk about the old times at home, my children just laugh at us. They look at us as though we are from outer space, the things that we talk about. The things we used to do and the things Mama and those did to us like wringing our ears or putting her fist in our forehead, I guess it was out of love and concern to discipline us and made better or appreciative people.*

Reuben McKenzie, though he married a black woman, felt superior to his neighbouring black Androsians. His house was built apart from his neighbours, with whom he seldom socialized. He also discouraged his daughters as they entered puberty from becoming too close to black boys.

Two of Marguerite McKenzie's older sisters, Louise and Doris, had moved to Nassau by the late 1940s, probably to avoid the pressure from young men in the village. It was the custom for a suitor after consulting his parents for their views about his intended and her family, to write to the girl's parents. The letter requested visiting rights and his intentions to ask for the young lady's hand in marriage. When engagement letters started arriving from admirers, asking for Marguerite's hand, Mr McKenzie decided it was time to send her to Nassau to "get away from the young men in Long Bay Cays". Despite his choice of bride, he did not approve of her marrying a black man.

Marguerite McKenzie, chaperoned by Mrs Lillian Bain from Bain Town, Andros, travelled to Nassau on a sailboat called *The Reliance*, owned and captained by Manassah Adderley. Her life would soon change dramatically.

2
Move to Nassau – Courtship and Marriage

Nassau as a single woman

The move to Nassau in 1946 must have been quite an experience for the 14-year-old Marguerite McKenzie. Unlike Andros, Nassau in the 1930s and 1940s had undergone some modernization. It had benefited materially from the Prohibition years between 1919 and 1933, and the growth of tourism during the 1920s and 1930s stimulated the expansion and improvement of the infrastructure and the building of hotels. Nassau by the 1940s had a reputation as a tourist destination and a seasonal resort for the wealthy and had also become known internationally as a tax haven, attracting foreign investment. Because of its loose tax structure – there were no income, profits, capital gains or real estate taxes – many investors were drawn to Nassau to escape taxation in North America, Britain and Canada. The expansion of tourism in the post-World War Two years, with its ancillary spin-offs in construction, finance, real estate and foreign investment, generated many jobs, especially in Nassau, creating a high level of prosperity and optimism.

Marguerite McKenzie lived with an older sister, Louise, who had moved to Nassau some years before. Louise's home was at first situated in Hospital Lane before she moved to Meadow Street and then to Augusta Street. Marguerite attended the Western Senior School, where she was considered a good student by teachers such as Doris Johnson, who was also destined for greatness. Marguerite left school at 16 and remembers that she performed the part of the mother of Jesus in a Christmas school play with Wakely Deveaux playing Joseph. Some of her schoolboy admirers gave her the nickname "Virgin Mary".

Her first job was with noted photographer, Stanley Toogood. His office was located on Bay Street near to Home Industries and Cole's Pharmacy, opposite the Royal Bank of Canada. She worked at Toogoods for a number of years, learning from Leroy Burrows how to develop black and white film. In fact Burrows had assisted her in getting the job.

Marguerite McKenzie met others at Toogoods such as Helena Lightbourn, Dorith Stockdale and Olga Roberts, some of whom have remained friends today. She recalls that Helena Lightbourn, who became a professional photographer, plucked her (Marguerite McKenzie's) eyebrows, which never grew back!

Knowing that she was from Andros, her co-workers were kind and showed her around Nassau. In the lunch hour they would walk around the town taking photographs. She believes "that is where all Mr Toogood's profits went – wasting the man's film". On an assignment with Leroy and the others, he took a beautiful photograph of her sitting on a wall dressed in a wide plaid skirt from the boutique Cinderella owned by Luxie Black and a sea-island cotton blouse from Distinctive Shops, owned by other members of the Black family.

After several years of employment with Toogoods she left but stayed in the field of photography. Her next job was with Colyn Rees, who married Helen Johnson. Mr Rees had a studio on the corner of East and Shirley Streets in the Johnson Building, now owned by lawyer and politician Mr Tennyson Wells.

There she met Andre Rodgers who later became the first Bahamian to play baseball in the major leagues in the United States. The baseball stadium in Nassau was named in his honour.

During her employment with Colyn Rees, she remembers the kindness of his wife, Helen. Mrs Rees "opened some doors for me" and started a charge account for her at Ambrosine, the leading dress shop, owned by Mrs Rosemary Appleyard. Stewarts, located on the corner of Charlotte and Bay Streets was another fine shop, which sold Amalfi shoes.

In about 1950, Marguerite Pindling earned £5 a week, which in those days went a long way. Money had to be carefully managed in order to pay bills. For example, she paid Ambrosine £1 a week. Marguerite Pindling did not spare herself where clothes were concerned. She was always elegantly and neatly dressed and was admired from this period onward. Her cousin Augusta Kemp Claridge, who was close to Mrs Appleyard, worked for Ambrosine and always assisted Marguerite when she visited the shop. Many years later, Mrs Appleyard renovated Ambrosine and asked Lady Pindling officially to reopen it. Another leading shop, selling sweaters and blouses, to which Marguerite Pindling was attracted was Amanda Furs, owned by Amanda Borer. Fortuitously, her sister Doris worked there.

For recreation, Marguerite Pindling watched movies at the Nassau and Capital theatres on Saturdays, after which she went to the Elbow Room in Bank Lane in the Boyle Building for milkshakes and hamburgers. On Sundays she attended St Agnes Anglican Church, a practice she continued.

Her friends at the time included Vernice Moultrie (Cooper), who lived around the corner from the Augusta Street house. Vernice Moultrie, a Government High School graduate and a friend of Lynden Pindling, worked at Telecoms and was known by everyone who had or needed a telephone. She and Marguerite McKenzie remained fast friends. Two other friends were Luxie Black who owned Cinderella, a clothing boutique, and also sewed for Marguerite, and Cynthia Rutherford who still sews for her.

Marguerite Pindling remembers that in the late 1940s and early 1950s there was some crime, but not violent crime. She states: "I used to walk home from the studio to Augusta Street at about 11 p.m. by myself. The streets were empty and dark." She did not yet have a car. Her sister Louise had a bicycle.

Courtship and marriage

It was fortuitous that Marguerite McKenzie changed jobs, leaving Toogoods to work for photographer Colyn Rees. Lynden Pindling's office was located in the Johnson Building, owned by Rees's in-laws, and there Rees kept his studio.

Obviously Lynden Pindling noticed Marguerite McKenzie, and their paths crossed at the post office. Marguerite Pindling recalls that she was sent to collect the mail. The Rees's box was "right at the entrance as you approach it from Bay Street". She was at box number 645 and heard someone say "Hello?" "I didn't look around because I didn't think he was talking to me because I didn't know anybody and didn't say anything. So he came back and said hello again and I didn't look around. That was the first time."

Lynden Pindling was persistent. "The second time he said hello, I answered with the same – then hurriedly retrieved the mail and ran back to the office wondering who this person was." They saw each other in the post office again and he passed the door where she worked. She was shy and when she saw his reflection in the pictures on the wall, she would go to the back of the studio and not answer when he called.

Finally, they spoke at more length and he asked her out on the following Saturday night. At first she refused. After the third attempt, he said "I'm not going to ask anymore." She was intrigued and accepted his invitation thinking she would "get rid of him". But soon they fell in love and agreed to marry.

The first date was not very romantic. Lynden Pindling borrowed a friend's car (the late Berkley Ferguson's) and the car broke down on a hill on the way to the Ardastra Gardens. Luckily a taxi driver by the name of Osborne Kemp passed and took them to their respective homes, hers in Augusta Street and his in East Street. "That's how it all began."

The courtship lasted from late 1954 to early 1956. During that time (in 1954), Lynden Pindling was hit in the left eye while playing baseball. He was hospitalized in the Bahamas General Hospital (renamed the Princess Margaret Hospital in 1955 on the visit of Princess Margaret) for about three weeks during which time eye surgeon Henry Steel-Perkins treated him and saved the sight in that eye. Marguerite McKenzie visited him every day and this endeared her to him.

She was loyal to him politically even in courtship. In 1955, a year before the 1956 election, Lynden Pindling registered himself as a voter for the City of Nassau on the grounds of having a lease on his office in the Johnson Building. When Colyn Rees found out, "he hit the ceiling" and Marguerite almost lost her job. The Johnsons, who owned the building, were upset that a member of the Progressive Liberal Party (PLP) was voting on their property. Marguerite overheard the discussion in which they decided to challenge Lynden Pindling's registration. He was appreciative of the information as it gave him time to prepare his legal arguments. Marguerite acted as go-between, convincing her employer Colyn Rees (and thus the Johnsons) that Lynden had a cast-iron case. In the event nothing more was heard and Lynden Pindling's vote in the constituency of Nassau City stayed unchallenged.

Lynden Pindling and Marguerite McKenzie decided to get married. This had its problems as their respective parents opposed the match. The McKenzies thought Lynden too dark and perhaps "too radical". Additionally, he had not approached them to ask for her hand in marriage as was the custom in the Out Islands. The Pindlings wanted a more academically qualified woman for their only son. In an interview with Professor Craton, Lady Pindling stated: "His mother was completely beside herself. I suppose it was because I was an island girl and didn't measure up to what they had in mind for their son. But then they did not know me. And I didn't know them, didn't get to meet them even till we got married."

Mr Pindling was angry because he was not involved in bringing them together. He thought he should be in charge. Dame Marguerite recalls: "You see, he was supposed to do everything for Lynden. Especially pick his wife. And then Lynden went and picked his own wife …".

According to Lady Pindling, Sir Lynden told her they were getting married at 6 a.m. next Saturday morning. Obviously they had discussed it. They were married by Anglican Father David Pugh at St Anne's Church on Fox Hill Road and East Bay Street, on 5 May 1956 during the campaign for the election of 8 June. The wedding party included Marguerite McKenzie's sisters Doris and Julie, who were maid of honour and bridesmaid respectively, Charles Albury, Doris's fiancé, Exumian and lawyer Livingstone B. Johnson, best man, and of course the couple, Lynden and Marguerite. A friend of L. B. Johnson's was also present.

The couple flew to West End, Grand Bahama that afternoon to collect some legal fees in order to finance the honeymoon. When they arrived in Miami all available hotels (Miami hotels were still segregated) were booked solid because of an Elks Convention. Fortunately, Lynden Pindling had a lawyer acquaintance, Mr G. E. Graves, living in Liberty City. He and his wife Ann put them up for the week.

While there, L. B. Johnson rang to give them the bad news that the cottage "Londonderry Cottage" located in the Pond not far from St Matthew's Church, that had been rented for them, was no longer available. The landlords discovered who the tenants were and refunded the rent. They were anti-PLP and did not want any PLPs living there. L. B. Johnson searched for other accommodation but to no avail. Landlords were either anti-PLP or were afraid to rent to a PLP for fear of being victimized. The young couple had no choice but to live with A. F. and Viola Pindling on East Street.

Marguerite had never met Lynden's parents and admitted she was shy and even scared on that Sunday afternoon when they arrived at their home. They spent the first four years of their marriage there. It was "an uncomfortable time" and she says that she followed Lynden around wherever he went because she was afraid if she stayed home, they might ask her too many questions.

3
A Young Wife – Work, Politics and the Coming of Majority Rule

Work

Soon after getting married, Marguerite Pindling in early 1957 quit her job at Colyn Rees Studio and worked for her husband. She took typing lessons with Ms Althea Mortimer in Meeting Street, to assist her as she took over from Lynden Pindling's secretary. She admits that she was "sure she didn't pass the test but Ms Mortimer gave me the certificate anyway".

Marguerite was able, however, to type all the correspondence, conveyances and company incorporations. At first the office remained in the Annex to the Johnson Building, before moving to Parliament Street in May Anderson's building opposite the Cenotaph. Later they moved to Union Dock and then to the Sassoon Building on Elizabeth Avenue and Shirley Street, which served until 1967. The office was small. L. B. Johnson, who previously was a magistrate, joined Pindling at first at Parliament Street and then at the Union Dock. Mr Johnson's secretary, Rosemay Saunders, left and was replaced by Rubie Livingstone, who later married Loftus Roker. Lady Pindling says that "Ms Livingstone was a competent secretary ... a G.H.S. (Government High School) graduate."

Politics – the 1956 election

A month after they were married, Lynden Pindling was elected to the House of Assembly for the Southern District, in New Providence. Marguerite Pindling, who had attended some rallies on the Southern Recreation Grounds and Windsor Park, describes the day of the election from her perspective:

> I remember he left home early in the morning. He might have told me but it didn't register because I didn't know what an election was and he was gone all day. I didn't know his family. They spent most of their time in their little petty shop and so I was at home alone. Then around 7–7.30 that evening I heard the noise and people shouting, coming up East Street from Wulff Road. I was sitting on the bed and I pulled the Venetian blind down, peeped

through one of the slats to see what was happening. As I looked through the slats the men brought my husband on their shoulders and they just landed him over the gate, over the fence and ... on to the pavement in grandpa's yard because the fence was right on the street and I ran outside and said, "What happened?" He said, 'I just got myself elected'... and that is how my (married) life began. It was 8 June, 1956 and the slogan was "On June 8th vote this way, Fawkes and Pindling all the way".

Lynden Pindling was elected as Parliamentary Leader for the Progressive Liberal Party (PLP) in the House of Assembly, H. M. Taylor having lost his seat. He became busy working at law on week days and campaigning both in New Providence and on the Out (Family) Islands at the weekends. He would often travel with the Chairman of the Party, Henry M. Taylor, Clarence Bain and A. D. Hanna to the Out Islands. In 1959 they visited Inagua, staying for eight days. Lynden Pindling also travelled to London with Henry M. Taylor and Milo Butler in October 1956.

During these periods Marguerite Pindling tried to keep herself busy in the office. By late 1956 the Pindlings had a car, a 1953 Ford, licence plate number 539. Previously, they were driven by taxi by a Bahamian called Biggie Taylor who drove taxi number 62 – he lived on Taylor Street. While her husband was in London (he was away for two weeks) Marguerite Pindling took her driving test. She remembers being taught by Mr Antonio and tested by Errington "Bumpy" Watkins who was then on the police force. As was the custom, during her test she was obliged to drive up Peck's Slope, which was a tricky hill to manoeuvre with a stick shift car. Fortunately, she passed her test on the first try but admits she could not reverse well and often dented the driver's side when attempting to enter the garage on Flint Street.

Besides helping her husband at the office Marguerite Pindling also assisted the PLP in raising funds. Living on East Street, she came in contact with many PLP women who lived in the area. She said that Mrs Effie Walkes took her under her wing and together with such women as Madge Brown, Ethel Kemp, Bertha Isaacs (later made a Dame) and several others, held many sales and picnics (called cookouts today) to raise funds for the Party. These were held in Mrs Walkes's yard on Flint Street on Saturdays and at the Montagu Beach, among other venues.

Children and a new house

During the four years at East Street, Marguerite Pindling worked very hard at the office. Lynden Pindling was very busy with law, politics and travelling. She felt it her duty to keep the office open and was able to save

1. Reuben and Viola McKenzie (Marguerite's parents) and her half-brother, Bertie

2. The house in which Marguerite McKenzie grew up in Long Bay Cays, Andros

3. The house Marguerite Pindling built for her mother in the early 1960s

4. Marguerite McKenzie eating a fruit on the back porch of her sister's house on Augusta Street, Nassau

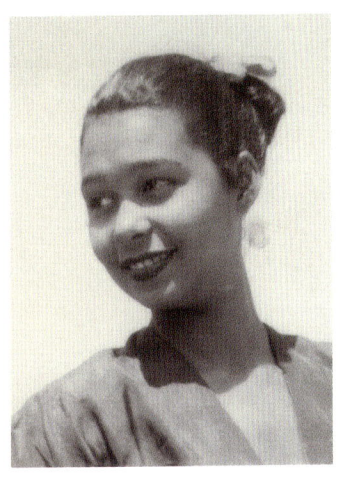

5. Marguerite McKenzie on the Market Wharf, Nassau

6. Marguerite McKenzie in her sister's house in Augusta Street, Nassau

7. Marguerite McKenzie at her brother's house in Virginia Street, Nassau

8. Marguerite McKenzie when she worked for Stanley Toogood Studios. Photo taken by her colleague, Leroy Burrows

9. Lynden and Marguerite Pindling leaving St Anne's Anglican Church after their wedding on 5 May 1956

10. The wedding party. From left: Mrs Doris Albury (née McKenzie), Lynden Pindling, Charles N. Albury (father-giver) Marguerite Pindling, Julie McKenzie Armbrister and L. B. Johnson (best man)

11. Lynden Pindling opens the door for his bride

12. Marguerite Pindling – a portrait by photographer Mrs June Stevenson

13. Lynden and Marguerite Pindling on Lynden Pindling's first day in Parliament, 9 July 1956

14. Leader of the Opposition Lynden Pindling and Marguerite Pindling at Clifford Park, 1964

15. Mr and Mrs Pindling with their children, Leslie, Obi and Michelle on the day Mr Pindling was sworn in as Premier in 1967; she is pregnant with Monique, her fourth child

16. Lynden and Marguerite Pindling with Cyril Stevenson and June Stevenson at the Saxony Hotel, East Street. *Photo: Maxwell Stobbs, Maxwell's Studio*

17. Official portrait of Mr and Mrs Pindling, 1968, at their Soldier Road residence

18. Marguerite Pindling in the 1960s. *Photo: Howard Glass, Ministry of Tourism*

19. Marguerite Pindling and Lynden Pindling with daughter Michelle and son Obi in the late 1960s. *Photo: William Roberts, Bahamas Ministry of Tourism*

20. Marguerite Pindling with her daughters Monique (centre) and Michelle (right) and their dog 'Sneeze'. *Photo: Howard Glass, Ministry of Tourism*

21. Mrs Pindling meets Mr and Mrs Roy Hamilton, late 1960s. *Photo: Eddie Deveaux*

22. HM the Queen, HRH the Duke of Edinburgh, the Speaker of the House of Assembly Robert Symonette, Mrs Diane Symonette, Lynden Pindling, Leader of the Opposition and Mrs Pindling and their son Obi Pindling, 1966. *Photo: Ministry of Tourism*

23. Marguerite Pindling with three of her children, Michelle, Leslie and Obi, early in 1967

24. Marguerite Pindling casts her vote on 10 January 1967. *Photo courtesy of the Estate of Dame Doris Johnson*

25. Marguerite and Lynden Pindling in Detroit, Michigan, 31 May 1962

26. Lynden and Marguerite Pindling return to Nassau to cheering crowds celebrating their victory in 1967. *Photo courtesy of the Estate of Dame Doris Johnson*

27. Lynden Pindling, Leader of the Opposition, being introduced to HM the Queen and the Duke of Edinburgh by Premier Sir Roland Symonette in 1966. *Photo: Roland Rose, Bahamas Ministry of Tourism*

28. Marguerite Pindling and Obi (her son) on the day of his christening, on the porch of his grandparents' house in East Street in 1959

29. Marguerite Pindling (centre) with Dorrith Stockdale (Grant), Mr Stanley Toogood, Leroy Burrows and Helena Bowe Lightbourn; Mr Stanley Toogood was her first boss

30 Marguerite Pindling with Leslie, Michelle and Obi in about 1964. *Photo: Leroy Burrows, Toogood Studios*

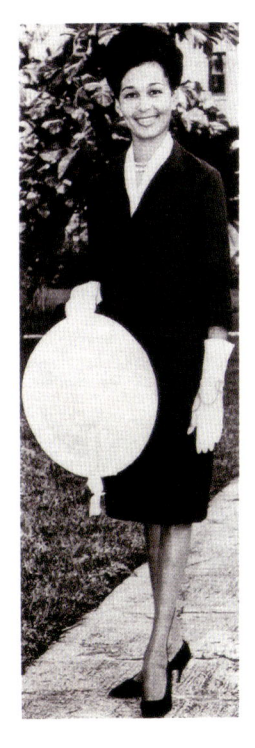

31 Marguerite Pindling in the gardens of the British Colonial Hotel, 1964. *Photo: Stanley Toogood*

32. Marguerite Pindling with Obi, Michelle and Leslie in 1967. *Photo: Frederick Maura, Bahamas Ministry of Tourism*

33. Lynden and Marguerite Pindling with their fourth child Monique at her christening. *Photo: Howard Glass, Bahamas Ministry of Tourism*

34. Marguerite Pindling at home with Monique a few days after she was born. *Photo: Howard Glass, Bahamas Ministry of Tourism*

35. Marguerite Pindling poses at the side of her portrait in the late 1960s/early 1970s.
Photo: Howard Glass, Bahamas Ministry of Tourism

36. Mrs Cindy Williams presenting her cookery book to Mrs Marguerite Pindling in the 1960s. *Photo: Howard Glass, Bahamas Ministry of Tourism*

37. Shortly after Independence. Standing: Sir Leonard Knowles (Chief Justice), Sir Milo Butler, Governor-General, Mr Lynden Pindling, Prime Minister. Sitting: Lady Knowles, Lady Butler, Mrs Marguerite Pindling. *Photo: Bahamas Information Services*

38. The Pindlings attend the opening of the Maura Lumber Company on Shirley Street, Nassau, early 1980s; right: proprietor Mr Michael Maura

39. The Pindlings enjoy an intimate moment in the 1980s

40. Mrs Joy Williams, chairman of Woman 85, presents a cheque to Lady Pindling for the Red Cross Society; Mr Lowell Mortimer, committee member, looks on

41. "There's a Brown Girl in the Ring" – Mrs Pindling dancing a ring play dance, late 1970s (dress by Androsia). *Photo: Bahamas Ministry of Tourism*

42 Marguerite Pindling with actress Rhonda Fleming, in Beverly Wilshire Hotel, Beverly Hills, California, 1970s

43. The Pindlings at the opening of Royal Bank House, late 1980s

44. Mrs Pindling with other Ministers' wives at Marlborough House, London, 1972. Thelma Macmillan, Zoe Maynard, Christine Francis, Lady Butler, Beryl Hanna and Marguerite Pindling *Photo: Howard Glass, Bahamas Information Services*

45. On the occasion of Sidney Poitier's honorary knighthood at Government House; from left: Sir Milo Butler, Lady Pindling, Sidney Poitier, Sir Lynden Pindling, Joanna Shimkus, Lady Isaacs, Sir Clement Maynard, Sir Kendal Isaacs, Lady Butler and Carlton Williams. *Photo: Bahamas Information Services*

46. Mr and Mrs Lynden Pindling at their 25th anniversary luncheon, 5 May 1981. *Photo: Toogoods*

47. The Pindlings and their children at the premiere showing of *Buck and the Preacher* at Nassau's Shirley Street Theatre. *Photo: Bahamas Tourist News Bureau*

48. Vernice Cooper, Zoe Maynard, Clement Maynard, Michelle Pindling, Marguerite Pindling, Winston Saunders, Gail Saunders and Mel Doty. At the Beaux Arts Ball. *Photo: Bahamas Information Services*

49. The Pindlings with Mr and Mrs Ted Arison at the opening of the Crystal Palace Hotel, Nassau, late 1980s. *Photo courtesy of the Crystal Palace Hotel*

50. Mrs Zoe Maynard, wife of the Minister of Tourism, Mr Ellison Thompson (Permanent Secretary) and Mrs Pindling. *Photo: Bahamas Ministry of Tourism*

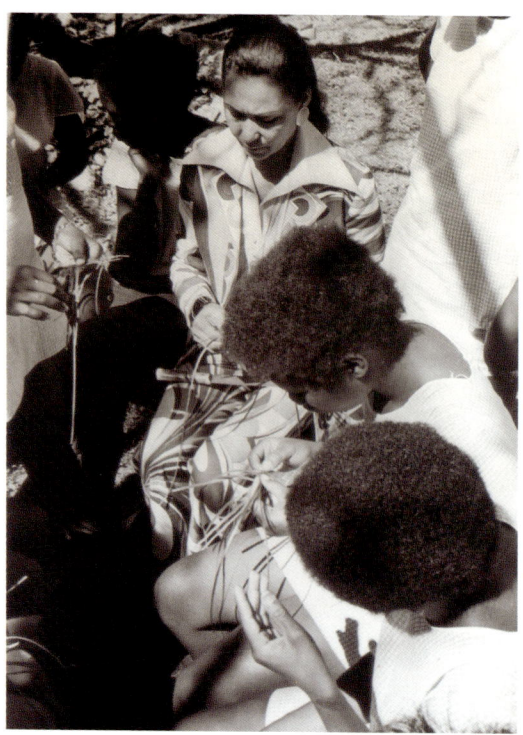

51. Mrs Pindling teaching the students of Andros how to plait at her home at Long Bay, Prospect Ridge, Nassau, 1970s. *Photo: Howard Glass, Bahamas Ministry of Tourism*

52. Mrs Pindling hosting a ladies' luncheon at the Balmoral Hotel in the early 1970s.
Photo: Bahamas Information Services

53. Lady Pindling with Bobby Symonette, former Speaker and son of the former Premier, and Lady Symonette.

54. HM the Queen greets Mrs Marguerite Pindling on a visit to Nassau in 1977. *Photo: Bahamas Information Services*

55. Mrs Pindling and Lady Cumming-Bruce in the Straw Market. *Photo: Bahamas Information Services*

56. A classic photograph of Mrs Pindling and HRH the Prince of Wales at the Independence Ball, July 1973. *Photo: Bahamas Information Services*

57. Mrs Pindling with Sidney Poitier and Joanna Shimkus in the Beverly-Wilshire Hotel in the early 1980s. *Photo: Howard Glass, Bahamas Information Services*

58. Mrs Pindling chatting with Harry Belafonte at a benefit performance of *Buck and the Preacher* in Freeport, Grand Bahama, in the early 1980s. *Photo: Freeport News*

some money, which assisted them in building their first home on some property on Soldier Road previously purchased from Mr Percy Munnings. They moved into their new house in 1960. About this time she befriended Vernice Moultrie and Patricia (Patsy) Fountain (now Lady Isaacs). Patricia and Lynden Pindling were friends. He had written to Patsy while she was in England to tell her that he had met "this lady he was going to marry and she wrote him back". Patricia agreed and Dame Marguerite admits that a friendship started, as "every time we meet, Lady Isaacs remembers and we talk about it". Marguerite also appreciated Patricia introducing her to gynaecologist/obstetrician Dr Trevor Jupp, who delivered all the Pindling children.

She was able while still living in East Street to attend Hubert Farrington's dance school on Shirley Street for about two years along with friends such as Vernice Moultrie Cooper, Luxie Black, Rosalie Austin, Ruth Bethel and of course the indomitable Meta Davis Cumberbatch.

The Pindlings' first child, a son, Obafemi ("Obi") was born on 11 February 1959. Lady Pindling explains that as he was learning to talk there used to be a lot of fights on East Street and some of the protagonists hung around A. F. Pindling's fence. "Obi would be wide awake and he knew those four letter words. Then when Obi began to walk and talk, those were the first words he spoke." She remembers thinking that "we have to get him out of here" and this prompted them to finish their house.

Finances were tight. The original furniture consisted of a bed, and whiskey and rum wooden boxes supplied by George McKinney from the Amber Room on Wulff Road were used as chairs. They had a two-burner hot plate, two knives and two forks. In order to buy furniture, they had to sell the 1953 Ford. Later they bought a brand new 1961 Ford, the first new car they ever owned.

The Pindlings' second child and son, Leslie, was born on 15 July 1961. Lady Pindling was still working in her husband's office. She was always trying to upgrade herself. A very good friend, Vernice Moultrie Cooper, registered her to take the Dale Carnegie Course, which was being conducted at the British Colonial Hotel. When Marguerite hesitated, Vernice Cooper said: "Yes, girl, your husband is a lawyer and one of these days you might have to speak somewhere." During one of the sessions Marguerite Pindling asked to be excused as she did not feel well. She says, "by the time I got home I realized that I was pregnant – with Michelle." That same evening she won a book from the Dale Carnegie Course, *Don't Grow Old, Grow Up*. The course she took, along with Carleton Williams, Clement Maynard and Raphael Cartwright and others, was entitled "How to Win Friends and Influence People" and she is grateful to Vernice Cooper to this day for her foresight and encouragement to her to participate in the course. It gave her much confidence, although she admits she is still nervous when she stands before an audience.

Michelle was born on 21 November 1962. Politically, it was an exciting time. Women voted for the first time on 26 November 1962. Lady Pindling voted at St Augustine's College. The Suffragettes, led by Mary Ingraham, Georgianna Symonette, Eugenia Lockhart and Mabel Walker among others, and mobilized by educator and activist Doris Johnson, had been campaigning for some years for the vote for women. They pressed for Doris Johnson to address the House of Assembly. Because she was not a Member of Parliament she was not allowed to address that body, but a concession was made and she was given permission to address Members of the House in the magistrate's court.

Exciting political developments

Marguerite Pindling, like many thousands of Bahamian women, voted for the first time in 1962. She regrets that she was unable to campaign for the 1962 election as she was pregnant with Michelle.

The PLP was encouraged by the gains made after the 1958 General Strike, which it supported. In fact the Bahamas Federation of Labour led by Randol Fawkes, the Taxi-Cab Union led by Clifford Darling and the Progressive Liberal Party with help from Lynden Pindling, who was legal adviser to the Taxi-Cab Union, united to stage the General Strike between 12 and 29 January 1958, closing all hotels, the airport, the Electricity Corporation, garbage collection and a number of Public Works departments.

Surprisingly, the Secretary of State for the Colonies, Lennox Boyd, personally visited The Bahamas after the Strike. No other person of that status in the Colonial Office had ever visited The Bahamas before. His visit resulted in important electoral reforms, including adult male suffrage, the abolition of the company vote and the reduction of the plural vote to two. Four additional seats in the House of Assembly were created in New Providence. These changes had a significant impact on constitutional and political development. Lynden Pindling, who soon eclipsed Fawkes as the crowd's hero, attracted a number of aggressive newcomers including Paul Adderley, Clement Maynard, Orville Turnquest, Jeffrey Thompson, Arthur Foulkes, Eugene Newry, Cadwell Armbrister and Warren Levarity, mostly dark-skinned professionals who identified more with Pindling than with Henry Taylor, the Chairman.

The 1960 by-elections were fought between the recently established (1958) United Bahamian Party comprising most of the white members of the House who were either merchants or lawyers, and the PLP, in a racially charged atmosphere, with resounding success for the PLP, which won all four seats.

Buoyed by these gains, the PLP was confident of victory in the 1962 general election and was shocked and surprised at the United Bahamian Party's overwhelming victory. The PLP maintained that although it won only 8 of the 33 seats in the House of Assembly, it had polled more votes than the UBP, which won 19 seats. Of significance for the PLP were Lynden Pindling's retention of his seat and Henry Taylor's defeat. This was the beginning of the end of Taylor's active political career. Lady Pindling remembers the disappointment of the 1962 defeat. She said that it was "looking so good" for the PLP. They were "out on Clifford Park celebrating victory", but soon learned the results.

The PLP then changed its strategy. At the Party's Eighth Annual Convention in 1963, Henry Taylor and Cyril Stevenson stood down from the chairmanship and secretaryship respectively. Pindling, elected Chairman as well as Parliamentary Leader, consolidated his position as the undisputed leader of the PLP.

Arthur Foulkes, Warren Levarity and Jeffrey Thompson among others formed the National Committee for Positive Action (NCPA), a pressure group within the PLP between 1958 and 1960. It was not convinced that the original founders were confident that blacks could actually govern. After the devastating defeat in 1962, the NCPA saw the need to convince the people that the PLP could indeed govern. They attempted to do this through education, public speaking and their own newspaper, *The Bahamian Times*, edited by Arthur Foulkes, a journalist formerly with *The Tribune*.

Constitutional advance

The United Bahamian Party, with some pressure from the Colonial Office in London, agreed to constitutional advance. The Secretary of State for the Colonies, Duncan Sandys, discussed the issue of establishing ministerial self-government, to which both parties agreed. A Constitutional Conference was held at the Colonial Office in London, opening on 1 May 1963. Representatives from the UBP, the PLP, the Labour Party, the Government, the Legislative Council and the House of Assembly attended. Meetings were spread over a three-week period. The new Constitution established internal self-government and the ministerial system of government. The British Government would remain in control of foreign affairs, defence and internal security. The Act to establish the new Constitution was passed in July 1963, coming into effect on 7 January 1964. Sir Roland Symonette became the first Premier of The Bahamas and Lynden Pindling, Leader of the official Opposition.

From this time, Mrs Pindling was becoming used to her husband's absences. She kept busy with her children and the home and staunchly supported him. When she was able, she took an active part in political activities.

The PLP changed its tactics after the 1962 electoral defeat, becoming more aggressive and confrontational. Dame Marguerite remembers being in the House of Assembly when Milo Butler (later knighted) broke the 15-minute rule and was warned by the Speaker to sit down. When he refused, the Speaker "named him". She recalls:

> After they named him, I dashed out of the House of Assembly and I ran all the way around Rawson Square. The straw vendors were there and this particular lady, I'll never forget her, Mrs Beulah Smith, one of Sir Milo's leading ladies from Bain Town, and I was shouting to the top of my voice: "They're going to put Mr Butler out of the House, you all come, you all come." I then got to the Churchill Building steps and Batelco workers were being paid their salary and it must have been a Friday, and I said to them: "They're going to put Mr Butler out of the House of Assembly" and I left them. I didn't know the people heard me and by the time I got back to the House the people had surrounded the House so the UBP could not get out of the House. At that point they [four policemen] had brought Sir Milo downstairs to the Square, outside the House.

Shortly afterwards Mr Hanna was named and two policemen brought him out. The second time they named Sir Milo, Marguerite Pindling and Beryl Hanna (wife of Arthur Hanna) were in the House of Assembly. Mrs Pindling left the House and went downstairs to the Opposition's room to use the telephone to let Cecil Wallace-Whitfield know that they were going to put Mr Butler out of the House, and to come down quickly. Unfortunately, Cecil was not at his office. She was still on the telephone, she recalls, trying to get Cecil at home:

> The next thing I knew Sir Roland came through the door to the Opposition room and Sir Stafford was standing in the doorway and as I turned around, I tried to close the door. Sir Roland stuck his foot in the doorway to prevent me closing the door and said: "You little trouble-maker, you give me this phone." I was scared as the devil. I said, "I am no trouble-maker, I am trying to call my office." I had to think of something quickly ... I don't know where I went after that incident, but I was scared and Sir Stafford was standing over Sir Roland, just to make sure I did not get on the telephone again. That's when I realized that they, the UBP, were serious and they were sizing up the PLP's

action by the wives being in the Chamber ... They realized that each time Mrs Hanna and I attended a meeting something was up and so we had to change our strategy.

Sir Roland telephoned some 14 years later and personally apologized to Lady Pindling for the incident.

Black Tuesday

Marguerite Pindling was also actively involved in the Black Tuesday demonstrations on 27 April 1965 over the issue of the redistribution of the Constituencies.

Black Tuesday was a carefully orchestrated incident. During a debate over the Constituencies Commission, with which the PLP disagreed, Pindling rose. He stated that the Government did not intend to discuss their objections and amend the draft; that although the PLP had tried to negotiate with the Premier, it seemed that it was Government's intention to "push the matter through". Stating that he could have "no part in it" and calmly walking over to the Speaker's desk, he picked up the Mace. At that point Milo Butler opened one of the eastern windows. Pindling declared that the Mace "is supposed to be the authority of the people of the country and the people are outside". At this point he threw the Mace out of the window into the crowded square below. Milo Butler followed his example, hurling out the two Hour Glasses, which were used to time speeches. The PLP members left the House singing the song "Amen". The PLP was for peaceful demonstration but needed something to shock the governing party.

Marguerite Pindling knew what was planned, and also that she should keep it close to her chest as only a small number of PLPs knew exactly what was to transpire. Her job for the Black Tuesday demonstrations was to collect the placards from *The Bahamian Times* on Bahama Avenue in the (southern) Grove.

> *I arrived in Rawson Square with placards and rested them down. Mrs Hanna joined me near the post which marked the Islands of The Bahamas. The people were lined on both sides of Bay Street. I said to Beryl, "They are not coming for the placards" – so she and I put on ours, then everyone came and took one.*

She describes the beginning of the demonstration:

> *My placard read "This ain't Selma". I think this was around the time when Martin Luther King was agitating for change ... and*

I think Daphne, Cecil's wife, wore one which read "This is the end of the UBP" ... *Sir Lynden led a group from East Street north to Bay Street, Sir Milo came from the west, (Arthur) Hanna and Sammy Isaacs came from the east and I think Spurgeon Bethel, Clarence Bain and Charles Rhodriquez and the rest came from the south ... and they all converged on Bay Street. And they marched down Bay Street, and I think they entered the House of Assembly wearing their placards; the wives didn't go upstairs, we had to stay down to sort of keep the people peaceful. Once the people saw us they knew that everything was under control.*

People were quiet; very well behaved. At that point Beryl Hanna, Daphne Wallace Whitfield, Esther Armbrister and I were in Parliament Street just outside the western door of the House of Assembly. The crowd was so deep we could not move too freely so we remained. We stayed in Parliament Street to keep that group of people calm. Cecil [Wallace Whitfield] was in and out of the crowds and he and Carlton Francis were on Parliament Street near the Bay Street area making sure that everything was under control, keeping the people calm until time. We were told that about 11 o'clock anything could happen and then Cecil came around to me and some of the religious ministers and said: "Man they taking long, hey?" I said: "Yes, we may not be able to control the people much longer, we might have to go up and see what is happening." I'll never forget and then it started to rain and we all started singing "There Shall be Showers of Blessing".

So it was Beryl Hanna, myself and Daphne in Parliament Street by the western door. So Cecil came over to me after eleven and I said "Man Cecil they're taking long, you have to go up there and see what's happening and give L.O. the sign"; because the people were getting a little agitated now and they had to move quickly. I never saw the Mace because from where I was standing I couldn't see what was happening on the eastern side or northern side of the House – too many people. However, I heard the shouting and I realized then that it was all over.

According to Sir Lynden, Cecil came up the stairs in the House of Assembly several times and eventually he gave him a note – "Now is the time" – and suddenly there were loud cheers and shouts as the Mace came falling from the eastern window, crashing to the pavement below.

I couldn't see. I heard the people screaming and they ran around to where we were and then someone came to us and brought us a piece of the Mace, I think it was the rod, and gave it to Beryl Hanna and me. Anyway, then the people started singing: "We Shall Overcome".

Now then, by this time what was the mood? Excitement – not a noisy excitement, you know ... not rowdy, not boisterous – peaceful and quiet. I was still on the Parliament Street side. I couldn't see the men because they came out of the House on the eastern side. As Sir Lynden came onto Parliament Street the men lifted him on their shoulders onto the top of the mail van where he spoke to the people. Sir Milo was on the shoulders of the men. Things moved quickly. The next thing I knew Sir Lynden and some ladies including Doris Johnson, Effie Walkes and Ena Hepburn were sitting in the middle of Bay Street. I'm still on the Parliament Street side now because the crowd was so thick you couldn't move. The next thing we know Magistrate John Bailey, the Irish Magistrate, started to read [the Riot Act] and I said to Beryl, "He's reading something from a piece of paper"... I remember that while they were in the House someone came and told us that the Riot Squad was stationed by the Central Police Station. Mrs Hanna and I walked over to Central Station to see for ourselves for she and I were together all the time. We walked in the back to see what was happening. I said "You all coming to lock us up, hey?" And in that group was a police officer, Errington Rahming from South Andros, who turned out to be the first police driver Sir Lynden had after we won the '67 election. We went back to Parliament Street and suddenly, the next thing I know, Cadwell Armbrister ran from the northern side of Bay Street into the Square by Queen Victoria's Statue, where Bailey, who was standing on something, was reading this page. Pindling said: "What is this you're reading?" and he said: "This is the Riot Act" and Cadwell Armbrister said: "You're not going to read this today." He leapt forward and Sir Lynden shouted "Come back here, no Caddie, come back." He had to restrain him; I'll never forget that. That was the only excitement. That was the only time it became a little boisterous.

Sir Lynden defused any hint of violence.

> *Afterward the crowd walked away from Bailey. I was sitting on Bay Street with Doris Johnson, Ena Hepburn, Effie Walkes, Esther Armbrister and the rest of the women. As matters were getting a little out of hand, Sir Lynden asked everyone to move to the Southern Recreation Grounds. People moved very quietly and very swiftly to the Southern Recreation Grounds. Not an incident that I know of – not that I can remember. No one was injured. It was very peacefully done and I said you know, the Lord was truly with us, still with us because anything could have happened that day.*

Dame Marguerite says: "We took our case to the United Nations." The delegation to the United Nations in August 1965 included Cecil Wallace-Whitfield, Rev. H. W. Brown, Milo Butler, Lynden Pindling, Doris Johnson, Arthur Hanna, Clarence Bain and Arthur Foulkes.

After Black Tuesday – only two years before Majority Rule in 1967 – there was a lot of excitement. Dame Marguerite states: "People were excited. They were able to feel the change. The UBPs were running scared and the people at that point were very supportive. So much was happening and I was on the move and as I said, in 1966 Lynden Pindling went to London for more talks."

Marguerite Pindling in 1979 related to *Image Magazine* her experience on a trip to Kemp's Bay, Andros in October/November of 1966 while her husband headed a delegation to the Foreign Office in London. She knew that he intended to run for Kemp's Bay, and took it upon herself to "fly there and inform the people in my neighbourhood of my husband's intention". She continued:

> *We chartered a sea plane, my Michelle and me, and we landed about two miles down in the Bight in Driggs Hill. Although the people saw the aircraft land in the water no one came to fetch us and it was rough and it was also getting late. Finally two men came in a dinghy and sculled us ashore, and then I had to walk from Driggs Hill into Long Bay (which is about three miles) with Michelle on my back. We stopped in every house in the settlement of Long Bay to let the people know that my husband intended to run for Kemp's Bay in the up-coming election which was scheduled for 10 January 1967. We arrived at my mother's house at about 10 o'clock that night and she was shocked to see me all soaked from salt water. The next day I met with all*

my relatives from the neighbouring areas and told them why I was there. Before my husband returned from his trip to London, I had things well on the way. Then on his first visit to Kemp's Bay when he arrived at my mother's house, the "stalwarts" were there and pledged their total support to him. They said they would be prepared to give him a chance only because he was married to their cousin's daughter [smiles]. Before this, my husband represented the South Central district in New Providence, but in 1967 the Party decided to send him to Kemp's Bay. He took quite a gamble but he won.

On 19 September 1967, Monique, my fourth child, came along. During the election campaign I was unaware that I was pregnant with Monique. The UBP dissolved the House while Pindling was in London in late November 1966.

The election was called for 10 January 1967. Campaigning had to be done over the Christmas holidays and a few days in January. Lynden Pindling was still away on Nomination Day and Sir Cecil and I went down to South Andros to put his name in nomination. At that point Mr Stevenson had switched parties and the PLP decided that the only way we could retain the PLP seat was if Lynden Pindling was to switch from a safe seat in southern New Providence to South Andros.

He did it for the good of the Party, and to save the seat while he was in London I had to go down and put his name in nomination. We went with two sets of papers in case they did not accept him, I would have placed my name in nomination for him. That was the first and only time I ever thought of running. The then Commissioner was Gomez. Stafford Gomez was his name, I'll never forget, in a house on The Bluff, somewhere on The Bluff. Stafford Gomez was from The Berry Islands.

At that point there were only two Representatives for the whole of Andros, from Mars Bay to Morgan's Bluff. Before the 1956 election the UBP held the two for 21 years.

Dame Marguerite, an Androsian, describes the campaign:

We were in South Andros for 12 days and there was no means of transportation and it was rough. I mean the campaigning was rough ... I had to introduce my husband to the people and after he had campaigned throughout the other Bahamian islands; we flew down in this one-engine plane, staying until after the election. That was the first time I had been on a one-engine plane. Every time I looked out the window I saw ocean and I ducked, not wanting to see outside, and remained in that position until the plane landed on this little strip in front of Las Palmas Hotel. [They made three attempts to land.]

We stayed at my mother's house, a cottage I built for her. Fortunately we built it down to the road, for it was easier for him to move around as we campaigned. We campaigned beyond Deep Creek, meeting people. We had to scull across the Creek in order to get to the settlement of Deep Creek. There is a heavy current in that Creek and the ferryman, by the name of Mr Finlayson, had to scull all the way out towards the ocean in order for the current to bring the boat back to the landing. Anyway those were the rough days for us; that was my husband's first time but it paid off. That's when we met this tall Prophet, as I refer to him, Reverend Euthal Rodgers, in this octagonal house on the Creek in Deep Creek and he told Sir Lynden he was going to win the election and he asked: "Why did you say that?"; "Because it is in the Bible. You come inside and I will show it to you." And sure enough, he got his Bible and in Exodus Chapter 12 and Verse 3 it says "on the tenth day of the first month"... however it went after that and Lynden said, "If you say so Sir, you are the man of God." He said: "You take my word for it." And sure enough on election evening, when we heard those results coming in by way of telegraph and radio, we knew we had won Andros. We got 100 per cent out of Driggs Hill and the people knew that we had won but you know they were still sitting there with their arms folded and I'm wondering why aren't they happy, but they waited to hear it on the radio. They wanted to hear the official announcement on the radio saying that the PLP had won and that Pindling had won in Andros. That's when the jubilation started.

The elections on 10 January 1967 ended dramatically with a tie between the PLP and the UBP. The subsequent support of Randol Fawkes (Leader of the Labour Party) and Alvin R. Braynen (Independent and former UBP) who held the balance, gave Pindling the majority needed to form a new government. Majority Rule had finally come.

4
Life as First Lady, 1967–1980s

The Progressive Liberal Party's victory in 1967 changed the Pindlings' lives completely. Dame Marguerite admits that on returning from Andros after the election, she felt very dehydrated from the heat and dusty roads there. She was amazed when someone showed up at her home and said, "You have to have a photograph taken." She exclaimed "Photograph!" She felt in no condition to have her picture taken as she was sunburnt and drained and her hair needed attention.

A police chauffeur-driven car was available from the beginning, and even after they had attended a function the policeman and car remained at the Pindlings' house, which was then located on Soldier Road. The car stayed parked and after some time she went out and told them they did not have to stay. The police said, "It's all right." The house was near to the street so there was little privacy. Curious supporters and tourists used to "wait across the street opposite our home until the Prime Minister returned home after a day at the office", so, as she recalls, "we had very little peace. I am not complaining – the people were very happy and wanted to share in the excitement. PLP supporters Audley Munnings and Percy Munnings and some others actually slept in the bushes opposite our home, 'keeping guard' out of sheer pride."

Dame Marguerite admits that on their return from Kemp's Bay after the election she hardly saw her husband. He was busy putting together his Cabinet and trying to persuade Randol Fawkes and Alvin Braynen to join his Government. Sir Lynden attended a myriad of meetings and often returned home late, exhausted but happy.

During all of this excitement, Marguerite Pindling discovered that she was pregnant. She and her husband tried to keep it a secret, but people began to speculate and somehow the press got hold of it and very soon the news appeared in the newspapers. The late Dame Doris Johnson, a highly educated Bahamian teacher, who later served in the Pindling Cabinet and was subsequently appointed President of the Bahamas Senate, acted as Lady Pindling's private secretary. Apparently, "Whenever Dr Doris Johnson came, she was laden with books on etiquette, and after three months she made the announcement in a press release that I was expecting a baby which was due in September".

Mrs Pindling, in an interview with *Image* magazine in December 1979, said that she "really wanted to continue working in his [L. O. Pindling's] office because I found the work fascinating, but then of course there was another role for me to play as the Premier's [later in 1969 Prime Minister's] wife and social hostess of our country."

She took her responsibilities very seriously but was also able to balance her role as wife of the Prime Minister and that of mother to her children. She admits that her "first obligation" was to her family. She was fiercely loyal to her husband and tried never to let him down. She states that she said and did things he had to correct with polite scolding, but he could always rely on her and trusted her. She was his best friend and confidante, accompanying him to most national events. She acknowledges that he did not say much and she had to learn by following him and through observation. She states: "He kept me in my place and I kept him on his toes." Some Bahamians believed her to be more of a politician than Lynden Pindling!

When the children were very young Mrs Pindling tried to curtail her travel, but her husband, the Prime Minister, travelled extensively. At some weekends when he was free, they would travel to Kemp's Bay as a family or charter a boat and sail down to his favourite place, Staniel Cay in the Exumas. She was devoted to her husband and children and her loyalty to Lynden Pindling was unquestionable. She supported him both politically and personally. At home she assisted the domestic help with mending and sewing buttons onto her husband's shirts, and sometimes cooked. Sir Lynden came home every day for lunch when he was in Nassau and shared in a family meal.

Marguerite Pindling told *Image*:

> We served Bahamian foods and cream of conch soup is one of my specialties. We have crab and rice made with coconut milk and fried, steamed or broiled jacks or grouper and native mutton from Exuma or Long Island, and of course guava duff for dessert ... someone referred to our kitchen as the Pindling Restaurant because we do turn out some fantastic and very tasty meals. We have our heavy meal at lunch time and a light supper in the evenings.

Mrs Pindling liked entertaining, especially "informal get-togethers with people I knew well". Sometimes her female friends would come and keep her company at weekends. "When the children were home from school they taught us the latest dances." Those get-togethers were informal and enjoyable. She and her friends would sit in the kitchen and chat, sometimes until very late.

Soon after the PLP's victory, Lady Symonette, wife of Sir Roland Symonette, first Premier of The Bahamas, wrote to Lady Pindling offering assistance. Lady Pindling remembers Lady Symonette as a "very gracious" woman – one whom she had observed as First Lady during the United Bahamian Party's tenure while the PLP was in opposition. Mrs Pindling admired Lady Symonette and her daughter-in-law Diane Symonette, who was Bobby Symonette's wife. She recalls that in spite of their political differences, both ladies were "very kind to me. They treated me with civility, not like most of the other wives of the United Bahamian Party, who looked at you and walked by you as if you were not there." She explains that Lady Symonette and her daughter-in-law were not "good friends" with her, but when they met, they were "cordial" and shared pleasantries.

Sir Roland and Lady Symonette, later in the Pindling administration, invited the Pindlings to dinner. The invitation had to be postponed as the Pindlings were invited to attend St Lucia's Independence celebrations. On their return, they were able to accept the invitation. Sir Roland was "very gracious" and jovial as he took them through his kitchen and confided that he often cooked himself. In fact he was a good cook. The Pindlings reciprocated and entertained the Symonettes at their home, Long Bay. Dame Marguerite remembers that it was on this occasion that Lady Symonette suggested that they send Michelle and Monique to school in Switzerland.

Bay Street, Nassau's main street and its environs, from the 1950s to the early 1980s, unlike today, had a number of fashionable and quality dress shops. Some of the more well-known women's dress shops included Ambrosine, Francise, Amanda Furs, Stewarts and the Nassau Shop. During her early years in Nassau, Marguerite Pindling could not afford to shop at the top shops but she always dressed well. She particularly admired Lady Symonette's style in clothes. Marguerite was known early on for her style. She liked skirts, blouses and Liberty prints. She recalls that in the early days, when she was earning only £5 (five pounds) a week, she would credit dresses from Elwood Donaldson's mother, who kept a dress shop opposite St Agnes Church. Mrs Donaldson was from North Andros and offered her credit. Because of Marguerite's small salary and the various bills – rent and food – she did not always have enough money when Mrs Donaldson visited on Sunday mornings. When this happened, Dame Marguerite says, she would hide to avoid her.

Later, as her financial position improved, Marguerite was able to afford more expensive clothes, and she bought many Pucci dresses which were in vogue in the 1970s and early 1980s. She also had clothes made at Luxie Black's establishment on the corner of Shirley and Frederick Streets. It was there she met Cynthia Rutherford, a seamstress who sewed for Luxie

Black. Lady Pindling remembers her beautifully sewn Sea Island Cotton blouses made from material purchased at the Distinctive Shop owned by the Black family. Cynthia Rutherford still sews for Lady Pindling today.

Marguerite Pindling admired the style of various film actresses such as Lana Turner, Elizabeth Taylor, June Allyson and Ava Gardner. Lana Turner in particular was elegant and glamorous. Marguerite made a point of observing these actresses' styles in clothes. She also read *Vogue* magazine and by 1967 had gradually accumulated a good wardrobe. Sometime after 1967, she found a dressmaker in a store called Wilma's on Miami Beach. The dressmaker, named Rosa Platas, had been an actress in Cuba before migrating to Miami. Her husband was a fisherman. Rosa sewed for Lady Pindling until her (Rosa's) death eight to ten years ago. She remembers that Rosa wore a lot of bangles. After she retired from Wilma's, she sewed for Lady Pindling from her home. She kept a mannequin the size of Lady Pindling so that in later years there was no need for fittings. Nearly everything that Lady Pindling wore after 1967 was made by Rosa Platas. Lady Pindling's clothes were never duplicated. She bought material at Harrods, Liberty shops and Allan's Fabrics just off Oxford Street and selected styles from *Vogue* and other magazines.

Perhaps the most celebrated dress was the fabulous one worn by Lady Pindling when she danced with His Royal Highness the Prince of Wales at one of the Independence Balls. The photograph of her dancing with the Prince was taken at the Emerald Beach Hotel. The dress was made of white cotedesoir "encrusted with faceted rhinestones along the front and back bodice". People enthused about the outstanding elegance of the dress and her beauty, and were enthralled when she danced with the Prince. The photograph of Lady Pindling and Prince Charles has become famous. Erica James, Director and Curator of the National Art Gallery of The Bahamas, included Lady Pindling's dress in an unusual exhibition of ball gowns in July 2006, entitled "Bahamian History through Couture". She wrote of Lady Pindling on 10 July 1973 (Independence night): "On this evening Lady Pindling set a standard that has impacted fashion in The Bahamas for the past thirty-five years. On every occasion the 'manner of her bearing' became a topic of discussion and she has never disappointed." Also displayed in that exhibition was the evening dress that Lady Pindling wore at the flag-raising ceremony at Clifford Park on 10 July 1973 when the Union Jack was lowered and the Bahamian flag hoisted for the first time.

Other ball gowns exhibited included ones from Lady Hermione Ranfurly, which was given to the art gallery, Lady Butler, Christianne Oakes, Lynn Holowesko, Judy Munroe, Lady Zoe Maynard and Lady Dorothy Cash. Accessories such as evening bags and gloves, which included some belonging to Winnie Moore Sands, were also displayed.

Erica James explained that:

This exhibition was organized with a clear understanding of how historically fashion has often served to materialize the oppression of women. However, it aims to also show how in the context of The Bahamas, fashion has also been used to liberate and give voice ... It is hoped that this small exhibition makes us more aware as a people of living history and the need to preserve and protect significant objects of seeming insignificance: photographs, paintings, furnishings, hats and even dresses.

Dame Marguerite has always dressed elegantly and has been described as a "fashion icon". When she accompanied Sir Lynden to the Commonwealth Heads of Government in Ottawa, she wore a dress decorated with rhinestones, and even Pierre Trudeau, then Prime Minister of Canada, said that "she shone like a star". She admits though, that "the gown I wore at the Queen's Dinner – I realized I should not have worn it because it was too sparkling, but no one told me that you should not 'out-dress' the Queen. I looked at her ladies-in-waiting and I realized you're suppose to be one step down."

Even before Marguerite Pindling became First Lady, she wore elegant, but simple and relatively inexpensive, tasteful clothes. Bahamian women noticed her especially after 1967 and took more interest in themselves and their appearance. Her influence on dress styles in The Bahamas has been profound. In 1964 Mrs Pindling was included among the ten best dressed ladies in The Bahamas. She is gratified that Bahamian women dress so well and take care of their appearance. Besides dresses, she always liked big hats. In 1972, while attending the Constitutional Talks in London, after one of the sessions, Mrs Esther Armbrister, wife of Member of Parliament Cadwell Armbrister and proprietress of Peggy's Hat Shop on Blue Hill Road, New Providence, took her to meet Mr Frederick Fox, as she was one of his clients. She subsequently bought hats from Mr Fox, one of the Queen's milliners, and also from Willie Ferguson of New York. He was a Bahamian who had moved to the United States and worked at the United Nations, and was a brother of Cephas Ferguson, who once served as chaplain at the prison. The hat Marguerite Pindling wore to welcome Prince Charles in 1973 was made by Willie Ferguson. In fact, she still has the hat, shoes and bag that she wore on that occasion. She recalls that in 1973, large sunglasses were in vogue. She admits that she did not realize that when meeting royalty, one should not hide one's eyes or face. Lady Pindling has always been one of the best dressed women in The Bahamas. She not only took care with her dresses and hats, but also her accessories such as handbags and gloves. The bag she carried at the flag-raising ceremony was made of satin, rhinestones and glass beads with silver detailing. The bag, along with the dresses worn at the flag-raising ceremony and the Independence ball have been preserved and, it is hoped, will eventually be exhibited in the planned Bahamas National Museum.

Dame Marguerite states that her clothes were "not all that expensive". Taking advice from her cook, Mrs Roberts, who said, "Just be yourself and wear what you like; don't let the clothes carry you, you carry the clothes", she did just that. It seemed that no matter what she wore it always turned out well and looked stunning. She knew what she looked good in and "the simpler the better". However, Felicia R. Lee, *Miami Herald* staff writer, wrote in June 1987, that she would become "an object of gossip, speculation, rumor and admiration … In Nassau, her critics call her 'the champagne lady' and josh about her drinking and alleged shopping binges. Her admirers point to the money she has raised for the Red Cross and other worthy causes."[1]

Stressing that Bahamian women took an interest in their appearance more than before, Dame Marguerite relates:

> *Elaine Pinder remarked to me once that when they knew we were going somewhere they would make sure to get out there early so they could see what I was wearing and they would applaud, giving their approval. Sometimes we'd be going out in the evenings and my husband would say, "I don't like that dress" and I'd say, "I'm not wearing it for you, I'm wearing it for the people." It made you feel good that the people showed appreciation for that … I remember the first time I wore white stockings. My children were in school in Europe so that was the style in that part of the world. When I attended a beat retreat in Rawson Square I wore these chalky whites because I couldn't find a sheer and they laughed at me. So the next thing I knew, everybody was wearing white.*

But Lady Pindling was more than a stylish lady. She was a wonderful ambassador for The Bahamas and did her country proud on the international scene. Perhaps the most memorable experience in this regard was in May 1980 when she accompanied the Prime Minister to London. Sir Lynden had been invited to chair the meeting and give the keynote speech at the annual ceremony in the Guildhall in London, honouring the winner of the Templeton Foundation Prize for Progress in Religion. Dame Marguerite recalls:

> *On arriving early on that morning at the Claridge Hotel my husband and I thought that he would get a nap before consulting*

with Sir John Templeton, chairman of the Foundation. Just as he slid under the sheets the telephone rang. At the other end was the late Rodney Bain, the Secretary to the Cabinet. Suddenly my husband sat up in bed, clutching the telephone. "What? When? How?" On putting the phone back on the cradle and taking one look at his facial expression, I enquired "Oh God! What happened?" He said, "The Cubans bombed and sank the Flamingo, killing four marines; I have to get back to The Bahamas. Get Mr Templeton on the line." Obeying without a word, I got Mr Templeton (later Sir John) on the line. My husband said, "Mr Templeton, there has been a terrible incident in The Bahamas which requires my attention. I am leaving right away. Would you accept my wife to read my speech, would you accept her in my place?" Sir John approved but I did not think I could do it. My husband said, "Oh yes, you can, just read what is on the paper."

Marguerite Pindling was nervous and began practising the 20-page speech. She remembers calling a friend, Winston Saunders, to ask his advice about the pronunciation of Solzhenitsyn, with which she was unfamiliar. He told her, take it syllable by syllable. She took his advice and the next morning, 13 May, she confidently delivered the address to the 700 invited guests. She recalls: "I gained my composure about five minutes into the speech when I recognized in the audience the late Lord Pritchard, a Nassau resident. Dale Carnegie had taught me to pick an object in an audience and speak to that object. Lord Pritchard was my object. I delivered the speech almost flawlessly, almost as if it was my own." The guests included the recipient of the prize, Dr Ralph W. Burhoe. Also present in the audience were some of the prize judges: the Dalai Lama; Inamullah Khan, Secretary General of the World Muslim Conference; Leo Tindemans, former Prime Minister of Belgium; United States Senator Mark Hatfield; and Yehudi Menuhin, the violinist and philanthropist. Those gathered were enthusiastic in their praise and applause. It was indeed a defining moment for Marguerite Pindling, who was grateful to her husband for having faith and confidence in her ability to deliver the address.

During the 1970s and 1980s, Lady Pindling involved herself in a myriad of activities, which she enjoyed and saw as the duty of the Prime Minister's wife. She busied herself in assisting various charities, in becoming a patron of the arts and sports, by attending church services and openings of the annual Archives exhibitions, encouraging women's organizations and educational institutions and assisting the underprivileged.

Lady Pindling's major efforts in charitable work were directed at fundraising for the Bahamas Red Cross Society, the subject of the next chapter. She also assisted other charities in various ways, including fund-raising. She remembers selling raffle tickets and generally assisting the late Shirley Oakes Butler, younger daughter of Sir Harry Oakes, who chaired the Crippled Children's Committee for a number of years. In those days the winning ticket was drawn in front of the old Cat and the Fiddle nightclub owned by the talented Freddie Munnings, Sr.

She was happy to assist the Ranfurly Home for Children as well, selling raffle tickets and taking part in fund-raising. She remembers walking to raise funds for the Council for the Handicapped. In May 1970 she walked with 600 others to raise funds for the Christian Social Action Committee. She also walked for the local Pilot Club after returning from London the night before. Amazingly, Lady Pindling completed 36 laps of the Queen Elizabeth Sports Centre at $100 a lap. The event was sponsored by the Grand Bahama Port Authority. She also raised funds for the Children's Emergency Hostel, the Hopedale School and Abilities Unlimited.

Dame Marguerite remembers her efforts at Cat Cay, when she was able to raise money from the winter residents who gave so generously that the monies were shared between 12 charities. She personally presented the cheques to the charities at her home, Lynmar. More recently, in 2003, she organized and chaired a committee to raise funds for the victims of hurricanes Frances and Jeanne. The prestigious group comprised Nancy Kelly of Kelly's Home Centre, Paul Thompson, former manager of the Lyford Cay Club, William Cash of Lowe's Pharmacy, Kyron Strachan, Lady Isaacs, widow of the late Sir Kendal Isaacs, former Leader of the Free National Movement and Patricia Francis. In a matter of four weeks, by working the telephones and holding a meal of $35.00-a-plate pea soup for 500 patrons at the Crystal Palace Hotel, they raised $25,000.00. A cheque for this amount was presented to the Honourable James Smith, Minister of State for Finance. The event was given much publicity; the committee appeared on talk shows and their generosity was appreciated by the population at large. Dame Marguerite admits that she enjoyed raising funds, to which she was accustomed through having raised money in the early years of the Progressive Liberal Party.

Politically speaking, she and her husband realized that the churches were important too. The Baptist communities were very supportive, having helped to bring the PLP to power in 1967. The Church of God of Prophecy congregations played a significant role in their loyalty to the PLP. Dame Marguerite remembers Rev. Kenneth D. Josey, who encouraged his congregation to "praise God" and "Vote PLP", when the Party was in opposition. Marguerite Pindling happily accompanied her husband as Premier and Prime Minister when invited to churches. Following the PLP's victory, the Church of God of Prophecy invited the Pindlings to all its conventions. Bishops Brice Thompson and Nathaniel Beneby (Mr Pindling's barber), supported the PLP, as did Bishop Josey at the Church of God, which they also visited and where they often spoke.

As First Lady, Lady Pindling spoke often to the Women's Convention of the Church of God of Prophecy and the Baptist Women's Convention. On Monday 20 June 1983 Lady Pindling addressed the Church of God of Prophecy's Women's Missionary Convention at its East Street Tabernacle. Adopting the theme "Let us go on to perfection", she spoke about Jesus' life, exhorting the congregation to "Go forward with Christ". She offered ways in which members could aim for perfection – in dealing with people, showing mercy, "doing justice", walking humbly, "giving a full day's work for a day's pay and striving for good family life". She ended by sharing Henry Longfellow's *Psalm of Life*. The fifth verse reads:

> Lives of great men all remind us
> We can make our lives sublime,
> And, departing, leave behind us
> Footprints on the Sands of Time.

She also spoke to other churches, including Ebenezer Methodist Church and Dixie Church on Wulff Road. Visiting such churches, she loyally conveyed any important news to her husband.

Marguerite Pindling was a patron of the arts. She often attended openings of art exhibitions and encouraged artists. She gave remarks at an art exhibition by Wade Taylor on Saturday 27 February 1982. Recognizing Wade Taylor's early efforts in the 1970s, and the fact that he received national recognition, she dubbed him one of the "New Bahamians" who had "demonstrated a profound sensitivity to our national feelings recurring when he selected the conch as the major theme in his works". She applauded him for his continued success and his "journey to establish himself as one of the most outstanding artists in our community". She then declared the exhibition, "The Mythological World of the Conch", officially open.

The Beaux Arts Ball, which was held annually from 1975 to raise funds for the Dundas Centre for the Performing Arts under the chairmanship of Winston Saunders, was a favourite of hers. She attended and was patron of most of these Balls, which became extremely popular. The Ball itself began at 10 p.m., but partying started with drinks and cocktails at a home of one of the guests. The ballroom was usually "resplendent with sumptuous decorations which continued the black and white theme". The Beaux Arts

Ball, also known as the Black and White Ball, began when the chairman of the Dundas, Winston Saunders, asked Mel Doty to make a contribution towards the renovation of the theatre. He said he was unable to do so but would chair a committee. He was the first chairman of the Ball Committee and remained on the committee for many years. The first meeting was held in Nancy Oakes's Queen Street home. Mel Doty and James Whitehead usually designed and mounted the decorations, which were spectacular. James Catalyn was very active in the early years, especially with the production of shows or cabarets. At the 1978 Ball there was a call for pledges of donations of chairs for the Dundas, and patrons responded generously. The Beaux Arts Ball, usually held the first Saturday in December, started "the season". Lady Pindling's presence at the Balls brought glamour and charm.

Lady Pindling attended most official openings of the Department of Archives (then headed by Gail Saunders) annual exhibitions which highlighted different aspects of Bahamian history. She accompanied her husband to the second Archives exhibition, "The Sponging Industry in The Bahamas", in 1974. She took an interest in all the displays, always seeking to learn more about the Bahamian heritage. Her presence brought excitement to the openings.

On 1 October 1983 she gave remarks and formally dedicated and opened the Loyalist Memorial Sculpture Garden at Green Turtle Cay, brainchild of Artist Alton Lowe who was assisted by James Mastin, sculptor. Lady Pindling gave the background of the Loyalist influx into The Bahamas and spoke of their contributions, which included the founding of The Bahamas' first newspaper, *The Bahamas Gazette*, in 1784, architectural heritage, the founding of businesses, notable exploits in politics and education and pioneering efforts in business and commerce. She noted that racial discrimination and racial segregation were fostered by the Loyalists but owing to "the dauntless efforts of the sons and daughters of the slaves of the Loyalists this is one aspect of their legacy that has faded into ashes, for today the sons and daughters of Loyalists and slaves enjoy this land as equals." Lady Pindling's bust, along with those of many well-known descendants of Loyalists, is featured in the garden.

Ever loyal to her husband, Lady Pindling often spoke in Andros, sometimes at various schools. On Sunday 8 November 1981 she gave the keynote address at the opening of the Tenth Annual Parent–Teacher Conference of the School Welfare Committee in Central Andros. It was opened by the Hon. Darrell Rolle, Minister of Education and Culture. During the year before the 1982 election similar conferences were held in North and South Andros. Prime Minister Pindling opened the one in South Andros and A. Loftus Roker, Minister of Works and Utilities, the one in North Andros.

Emphasizing the need to introduce a re-education programme in traditional Bahamian values for both parents and students, Lady Pindling stated: "There is a need for increased social services to assist the disabled, the homeless, the lonely and the forgotten all over The Bahamas ... Our job is never done."

During the following year, on 16 June, Lady Pindling spoke at the speech day ceremonies at the South Andros Senior High School, urging the students to prepare themselves properly to take full advantage of the many opportunities that would become available. But she reminded them that in order to do well, it was necessary to "spend long and regular hours doing your studies and paying careful attention to both class-work and homework". Lady Pindling exhorted them to never give up and to commit themselves to "the pursuit of excellence", emulating the lives of great men and women and "above all, commit yourselves to succeeding by deciding not to give up when faced with problems and difficulties".

Lady Pindling was instrumental in encouraging the women of The Bahamas and the Progressive Liberal Party. In 1969, two years after winning the government, she hosted more than 70 delegates who attended the second Annual Women's Conference. Some years later in October 1981, she addressed the Business and Professional Women's Organization (BPWA), urging them "to strive more to reach out to all women of the Bahamian community", thus publicly focusing some attention on issues that affected daily the lives of the broad mass of Bahamian women.

Several businesswomen including Beverley Brice, Marietta Gibbs, Helen Astarita and Winifred Pedican were honoured. Also recognized were two women, Phyllis Aldridge and Emmabelle Hanna, who distinguished themselves in their work with the disabled. A final award was presented to Sheila Tracy, President of the BPWA, for her dedication in the organization and her efforts to create equal opportunities for Bahamian women.

Lady Pindling usually hosted PLP women during the Annual Convention of the Party. She also attended luncheons and events to honour women. One such event was a luncheon in honour of the Women's Suffrage Movement at the opening of the Women's Conference in December 1987.

In May of 1981, the year before the next general election, 40 PLP women were honoured for dedication and hard work. One of the women honoured, Isadora Maynard, wife of the national chairman, Andrew "Dud" Maynard, suggested during the occasion held in the ballroom of the Britannia Beach Hotel, "that six women should be nominated to participate in the upcoming general elections". The year before, a similar "challenge was made by Mrs Gladys Manuel, educator and Vice-chairman of the Women's Branch of the PLP". Gladys Manuel, during the Party's Twenty-fifth National General

Convention held in the second city, Freeport, Grand Bahama, noted that "The time has come for women of this country to take their places on the stage of the 'Handle It Express'." She urged that women should be elected to seats in the House of Assembly.

Mrs Marguerite Pindling and Mrs Beryl Hanna presented certificates of appreciation to the deserving women. Dame Marguerite, looking back to the earlier years, notes that "during those days I had the opportunity to laugh with the PLP women and to cry when they cried." It is not certain whether she was in favour of women running for office. She may, like the majority of Bahamians, have seen women as the homemakers and appears to have been equivocal about women holding political office.

In an interview with Basil Smith, contributing editor of *The Bahamas Review* magazine, which featured Lady Pindling on its cover as 'Woman of The Year' she stated: "Bahamian women have moved up the success ladder in so short a time that I personally felt that they have become more interested in their professions than family life. I have nothing against professional women – I am proud of them; but I am more proud of the professional mother and wife."

Marguerite Pindling reiterated these sentiments in an address to the Mothers' Club on Mothers' Day on Sunday 9 May 1982. First she paid a special tribute to the founding President of the Mothers' Club of The Bahamas, the late Mrs Frances Butler, known to many as "Mother Butler", who in addition to establishing the Mothers' Club in 1928, gave the nation one of its first legitimate national heroes in the person of her son, the first Bahamian Governor-General of The Commonwealth of The Bahamas, Sir Milo Boughton Butler. Then she invited the Mothers' Club, which undertook the task of feeding and clothing the underprivileged, counselling the youth, and in short, restoring traditional values, to assist in reversing the trend of lawlessness and indiscipline and the breakdown in the family structure:

> *Mothers today have soared to heights in the professional world of business and government that only yesterday were beyond our wildest dreams. Mothers are heading departments, leading businesses, pouring concrete, pumping gas and piloting planes. Mothers are, indeed, flying high. But at what price?*
>
> *Today, just when the challenges of motherhood are greatest, eleven, twelve and thirteen year-olds are having babies. No child this young that becomes a mother can hope to contribute to solving the problems of our society. Far from being a part of the solution, such a mother becomes part of the problem. We*

will never solve our problems so long as children are having children.

Mothers, especially, need to pay greater attention to how they raise their sons. We must now, more than ever, teach our sons that they are accountable for their actions and deeds. Sons must be taught pride, they must be taught a code of honour, they must be taught a respect for duty, and they must be taught all this while they are young. If a mother bends her young man to his duties as a son, he will never depart from his responsibilities as a father.

Today's mothers have, indeed, achieved great things outside the home. But, even in the face of all these achievements, no mother can afford to relax. No ma'am! A mother's work is never done. This is no time to pat ourselves on the back. Instead, we need to dig in and to build on our accomplishments so that our success inside the home can match our achievements outside of it.

It is our duty, as mothers and as Bahamians, to ensure that our children develop the highest sense of Christian ethics, moral responsibilities and self-discipline. These qualities are essential ingredients in the production of good, responsible and productive citizens which in turn, are the only assurances to the development of a good, productive and progressive nation. We, the mothers of this country, must regard the restoration of those positive traditional values as our principal task for the decade of the eighties. We must, in the words of the Prime Minister in his Convention address, "teach our children that if they do wrong they must pay for it sooner or later. If they expect consideration they must show consideration, if they want mercy, they must show mercy ... If we as parents fail to do our duty and live up to our responsibility we will make the job of the State harder than it should be ... Our value system needs to be put back in proper perspective."

I cannot think of a time more appropriate than Mothers' Day, nor a forum more suitable than a collection of concerned mothers, to invite Bahamians everywhere to focus attention on a growing problem in our community, a problem which the Prime Minister has described as a "crisis in human relations". The changing quality of relations between parents and their *children, which, if allowed to deteriorate any further, might pose a national threat to the stability of our society and, consequently, an obstacle to the continued progress and development of our beloved Bahamas.*

At no other time in the life of this Nation have so many mothers been pushed in so many directions, by so many different forces. City life, personal fulfilment, individual freedom, social and professional success and the declining significance of the family are all combining to assault ourselves and our homes, and to move us to neglect our children. But our children need us. They need us today more than yesterday and tomorrow more than ever. They need us desperately. Our children sing a song called "The Greatest Love of All", some of the words to which are:

> I believe the children are our future
> Teach them well and let them lead the way
> Show them all the beauty they possess inside
> Give them a sense of pride to make easier
> Let the children's laughter remind us, how we used to be.

Throughout our history, the mothers of the Bahamian community have been the most dominant force in shaping our society and contributing to the stability, growth and development of our major social institutions. It was their unselfish love for and dedication to their offspring which accounted for the many and sometimes painful sacrifices they had to make to ensure a better tomorrow for the sons and daughters of The Bahamas.

Our mothers, in expressing their hope for a better and brighter future, provided this Nation with a solid spiritual, emotional and moral base which formed the foundation for the just, free and democratic society we have in The Bahamas today. That tradition of love and respect for each other, discipline, hard work, gratitude and generosity in our relations with each other, should continue to be the essence of the Bahamian personality. We, the Bahamian mothers of today, must make it our personal responsibility to safeguard that tradition and to protect it from those forces that may seek to destroy it. In so doing, it would seem to me that we would be paying the highest and most sincere form of tribute to the mothers of our Bahamian Nation.

5
Lady Pindling and the Bahamas Red Cross

Immediately after the swearing-in of Sir Milo Butler as the first Bahamian Governor-General in August 1973, Mr and Mrs Lynden Pindling left for Ottawa to attend the Commonwealth Heads of Government Meeting. Mr Pierre Trudeau was then Prime Minister of Canada and a good friend of Lynden Pindling, having been introduced to him by Dick Birch, a former Canadian paratrooper and owner of Small Hope Bay in Andros. Pierre Trudeau frequently visited Small Hope Bay to scuba dive and met Lynden Pindling, who participated in the same recreation.[1]

Her Majesty Queen Elizabeth II attended CHOGM as Head of The Commonwealth. Lady Pindling remembers that she was presented to Her Majesty at the state dinner held at the Governor-General's residence in Ottawa. When it was her turn to be presented, she admits that she thought she could walk up to the Queen and start talking. She learnt otherwise. Her Majesty on this occasion asked her "What social work do you do?" "Somehow God was with me and I said, 'None Ma'am, but on my return to The Bahamas I shall become involved.'"[2] And this she did.

As a worldwide organization, the Red Cross was started in 1863 by a Swiss philanthropist, Henri Dunant, who organized help and assisted in rescuing the war wounded. Mr Dunant recorded his experience at the Battle of Solferino from a humanitarian perspective and then organized a committee to care for the wounded. His courage and conviction led to the establishment of the Red Cross. In 1867, the first International Conference of the Red Cross led to the establishment of the Red Cross as an independent and private institution.

The Red Cross was first established in The Bahamas in 1939 at the beginning of the Second World War, becoming known as the Bahamas Branch of the British Red Cross Society. Its main objective at that time was to promote comfort and relief supplies to members of the allied forces who were stationed overseas and on New Providence.

The Bahamas occupied a strategic position in the Atlantic hemisphere. Under the Destroyer-Base deal in September 1940, United States President Franklin Roosevelt in an Executive Agreement promised to turn over

50 destroyers to Britain. In return, Britain gave sites for bases to the United States on Newfoundland and Bermuda for 99 years and granted rent-free leases for 99 years on six additional sites ranging from The Bahamas to British Guiana (Guyana). The Bahamas base was on Exuma Island.

Additionally, in view of the menacing Axis submarine campaign in the Caribbean and the Florida Straits, New Providence, on which Nassau is located, was chosen to be the site of an Operational Training Unit under the joint auspices of the British and United States Governments. The building of the installation was supervised by the United States Army engineering department and an American firm, Pleasantville Incorporated. Work began on 20 May 1942 on two sites. One was just south of Grants Town, the predominantly black section of Nassau, at the site of a small landing field, the first in New Providence, that had been developed by Sir Harry Oakes, the wealthiest man in the British Empire, who had settled in The Bahamas in 1934. The other site was located in the Pine Barren near the western end of New Providence. They were called the Main Field and Satellite Field respectively, and collectively the "Project". While the Main Field would become Oakes Airport, the first commercial airport in The Bahamas, Satellite Field became Windsor Field and later the Nassau International Airport, renamed the Lynden Pindling International Airport in 2006.

The "Project" employed over 2,000 Bahamian men, many of them from the Out (Family) Islands, who had flocked to Nassau during the previous decade in search of jobs. While creating thousands of wartime jobs, the "Project" also created the background against which the Burma Road Riots occurred in June 1942.[3]

While the project progressed, British Royal Air Force personnel for the Coastal Command Service were being trained in the salubrious climate of The Bahamas, which allowed for much visibility. As Paul Albury noted: "The thousands of trainees who came here were not new to aeroplanes and the sky. Already familiar with single-engined aircraft, the 'conversion courses' at Main and Satellite Fields were designed to acquaint them with intricacies of two-engined Mitchells and four-engined liberators."[4] More than 3,000 officers and men were on the permanent staff of the Operational Training Unit (Number III), turning out over 5,000 trained pilots, "constituting more than 600 crews". On completion of their training, they left The Bahamas taking their aircraft with them, and "joined the Coastal Command squadrons in Britain, the Azores and Iceland".[5]

The Bahamas Red Cross was first presided over by Lady Dundas, wife of the then Governor. She was soon to be replaced by the Duchess of Windsor, wife of former King Edward VIII, who had been created Duke of Windsor after abdicating in order to marry Wallis Simpson. His exile had taken him to France, then Spain and finally to Portugal. The discovery of a Nazi plot to use the Duke to serve German ends, and possibly restore him to the throne, made it imperative for the British Government to get him out of Europe.[6] British Prime Minister Winston Churchill offered Windsor the Governorship of The Bahamas, a distant outpost, which he reluctantly accepted. The Duke and Duchess of Windsor arrived in Nassau on 17 August 1940.

On their arrival, the Duke of Windsor consented to be the Patron of the Red Cross and the Duchess, who hated The Bahamas, was appointed its new President. Such a prestigious and patriotic institution soon attracted a large membership. Its 189 life and 300 regular members were mainly upper-class white ladies, who met at the Red Cross Centre in George Street. Mrs Kenneth Solomon served as the first Senior Deputy President of the branch, while Mary Moseley, proprietress and editor of *The Nassau Guardian*, a pro-establishment newspaper, was elected Deputy Chairman of the Council. Mrs Ethel Adderley, wife of Alfred F. Adderley, prominent black lawyer, parliamentarian and civic leader, was the only coloured regular member in the early days of the organization.[7]

Non-whites were included among the nearly 500 associates and working members, enrolled not only from New Providence, but from nearly every Out Island in The Bahamas. About 44 working groups, organized by churches of all denominations, public schools, garden clubs, the Humane Society, the Mother's Club, the Young Women's Christian Association (YWCA) and a group of young women calling themselves the Woolgatherers, contributed.[8]

Numerous private individuals, both in New Providence and on the Out (Family) Islands, assisted, especially in sewing and knitting. Nearly a third of the knitted and sewn garments sent to England were made in the Out Islands. Bahamians patriotically contributed and gave unstintingly of their time to the work of the Red Cross.

The Red Cross in October 1940 also cared, along with the hospital, for two young British seamen, Roy Widdicombe and Robert Tapsscott, survivors of an Allied ship, the *HMS Anglo-Saxon*, which had been sunk in the Atlantic. They had miraculously survived a 3,000-mile transatlantic voyage over ten weeks in a small open lifeboat. Members of the Red Cross and Bahamians in general were made aware of the grim realities of war.[9]

In addition to shipping woollen and hospital garments, surgical supplies and children's clothing to England, the Bahamas Red Cross raised funds for various organizations in Britain and America. The Society sponsored tennis exhibitions, dances and a fair in the grounds of Government House. The Red Cross fair became the organization's main annual fund-raising event. It was also an attractive social outing, especially for the elite.

Marguerite Pindling's involvement in the Bahamas Red Cross Society began in 1976. At that time, Mrs Rowena Eldon, widow of Mr Sidney Eldon who had served as Comptroller of Customs, and mother of Anglican Bishop Michael Eldon and first President of the College of The Bahamas, Dr Keva Bethel, was the President of the Bahamas Red Cross. She was the first Bahamian to hold that post, while Mrs Lottie Tynes was the first Director-General of the Bahamas Red Cross. Mrs Eldon wrote a letter to Mrs Pindling asking if she would consider chairing the fund-raising events. She did not reply at once, as she had to get her husband's approval. When Mrs Eldon called to see if she had given any thought to the request, she accepted.

In post-war years, the work of the Red Cross was supervised by field officers from Britain. They felt the need to appoint their own director, which was realized in 1970.[10] By an Act of Parliament, in 1973 it had become a national organization known as the Bahamas Red Cross Society. A steering committee was appointed to guide the branch through all stages and this ultimately led to national status in 1973. On 14 December 1976 the Society became the 123rd member of the International Red Cross and during May of the next year, it became a member of the League of the Red Cross and Red Crescent Societies.

The national fair was the largest fund-raising effort for the Red Cross when Marguerite Pindling became involved. It was popular, being held in the Government House Grounds, and everyone looked forward to attending it. In those days the fairs were not very elaborate and were held only in Nassau, New Providence. Lady Pindling was determined to take the Red Cross to the people in the Family Islands as they traditionally had made contributions to the Society and should be allowed to continue to contribute towards its operation. Lady Pindling persuaded Mrs Eldon and Mrs Tynes that fairs should be held in the Family Islands and in 1977, the Society's Executive Committee agreed. Lady Pindling reminisces:

> That move was a very excellent one and of course it gave people on the Family Islands something to which to look forward and it was very exciting. The response that we received from establishments, the accommodations, everything was complimentary. I was able to use ... I don't remember whose aircraft we used, but it was complimentary. They took us and collected us. Mrs Eldon was a delightful soul to work with. She kept us in stitches, so much so, every time I hear the song "When I Survey the Wondrous Cross" I remember her. We were at the airport in Governor's Harbour when it was being sung on the radio and then she had a favourite saying, "When you see a chair, sit in it because you don't know

when you will see another one." I'll never forget that. She would sit there with her purse and take out this little plastic container and say "Child, this is my Valley of the Dolls." She had tablets in each little vial in these compartments and she would sit there and take them. I certainly enjoyed her company.

Lady Pindling, Mrs Eldon and Mrs Tynes, whom Dame Marguerite describes as "always very quiet", travelled to most of the Family Islands. The first fair held out of New Providence was in Freeport, Grand Bahama, in 1977. It was chaired by Mrs Rubie Nottage, wife of Kendal Nottage, a Member of Parliament at the time. She was assisted by Rev. C. B. Moss. The fair was a tremendous success. Dame Marguerite admits: "The expats there all pitched in and of course Mr Edward St George took it over completely and gave us everything we needed." There was one sad note, however. The husband of one of the helpers who was assisting them took ill and died at the Red Cross fair. Despite the success of the fair, Dame Marguerite admits that she felt guilty.

While she praised the Grand Bahama Red Cross members, there were some in that organization who questioned why the money raised in Freeport should go back to Nassau. Mrs Pindling explained that the money raised at the fair was for the Bahamas Red Cross Society, which is a national society. But money raised from the Black and White Ball which was held in Freeport, would stay in Grand Bahama.

Fairs were also held in Abaco, Acklins, Andros, Bimini, Cat Island, Eleuthera, Exuma, Inagua, Long Island and San Salvador. Thousands of people supported the fairs and hundreds made contributions of money to the Bahamas Red Cross. At every opening Lady Pindling spoke and was always complimentary towards the people of the particular island. In Cat Island in April 1983 she praised the island "for its rich musical heritage, the pride and patriotism of its citizens and the island's deep religious fervour ... the generosity of its people". She continued that while Cat Island is "not The Bahamas' richest island, its belief in a commitment to a strong community is unsurpassed".

Lady Pindling on 27 May 1983 at the opening of the Bimini fair, described it as "an exciting, interesting, refreshing place ... It's refreshing because of the unbeatable warmth and infectious personality of those who live here." San Salvadorians on 28 May were praised as being "among the most generous of The Bahamas ... You believe in yourselves, you believe in helping one another. That impresses me!"

Often there were two or three fairs in one island, but in different settlements. In Long Island in 1984 a fair was held in Clarence Town on

Friday 30 March and another one on Saturday 31 March in North Long Island. In her opening remarks Lady Pindling reminded the people in both settlements that disaster had "no respect for personages" and did not discriminate. "It strikes fiercely and often leaves in its wake many broken and sometimes shattered lives. It is at those times that the Red Cross is expected to step in and help quickly and effectively."[11]

One year, there were three fairs in one day (Saturday) in Andros – Nicolls Town, Fresh Creek and "down South". Dame Marguerite remembers:

> *My husband was manning that one for us – Kemp's Bay. Mrs Tynes and those were wondering how things were going down South. They wanted to know if they were making any progress. Commissioner Gray was there, so I asked him if he thought that Autec would assist us with some means of transportation and he said he would ask because that was kind of out of the ordinary. So he said to give him some time and after they received clearance they allowed one of their helicopters to take us down.*

A helicopter was necessary as you cannot drive all the way there because of the bights. Fortunately, accommodations for Lady Pindling and her entourage (which was sometimes large) were always complimentary, as was transportation.

The Bahamas Red Cross started the School for the Deaf in 1965 with the help of the British Red Cross in a building built for the school on Pitt Street. After some years the Government began to pay the teachers, and eventually took over the school.

Between 1976 and 1992, the Bahamas Red Cross raised over $2 million. Functioning on an annual budget of $350,000, the Red Cross Society in 1987 operated a meals on wheels service that served 9,000 meals a year; a home help service that cleaned more than 700 homes for the elderly and handicapped; a transport and supplementary ambulance service, provided on demand; a school milk scheme that distributed 1,500 half-pints of milk; a day-care nursery assistance programme for mothers who could not afford to pay for the care of their children; Silver Circle Clubs which served refreshments to senior citizens; a day rehabilitation centre with a membership of 35 handicapped persons who received a hot lunch three times a week; and a Centre for the Deaf. Transport was provided for the students each day. In 1987, Mrs Marina Glinton was Director-General and Mrs Frances Ledee President.

Lady Pindling was very instrumental not only in raising most of the funds but also in acquiring the land on which the new headquarters was constructed.

Mrs Rowena Eldon was concerned about the cramped headquarters at Longley House on Dowdeswell Street. She asked Lady Pindling to speak to Lady Eunice Oakes, widow of the late multi-millionaire Sir Harry Oakes, who was mysteriously murdered in 1943. At first, Lady Pindling hesitated. She recalled that when she was single she remembered "this elegant lady driving a station wagon and she would have her arm outside – a gloved hand. This blue-eyed lady would be looking at me and she would turn into Parliament Street every morning at a particular hour."[12] She stood in awe of Lady Oakes. Finally she agreed, and along with Mrs Eldon and Mrs Tynes visited Lady Oakes at Dale House to ask for property for the Bahamas Red Cross. Lady Pindling remembers that Lady Oakes at their first meeting said: "Now you know, I used to see you walking up Shirley Street and I always thought you would be somebody."

Lady Oakes agreed to give the Red Cross the property and the Society promptly erected a sign to say "Future Home of the Red Cross". But, as Dame Marguerite recalls, "The next thing we knew I was called to say the sign had been damaged" by a family which said it owned everything in that area. Lady Pindling along with the President and Director-General again visited Lady Oakes, who apologized and promised to find another piece of land for the Red Cross. It was located on John F. Kennedy Drive on which the new headquarters was built.

At the official opening of the new Red Cross Headquarters on 15 July 1983 Lady Pindling delivered these remarks:

> *Madam President, Lord Bishop, Madam Director-General, Past Presidents Mrs Rowena Eldon and Reverend C. B. Moss, Past Director-General Mrs Lottie Tynes, Distinguished Guests, Ladies and Gentlemen:*
>
> *We have reached a glorious point in the history of The Bahamas Red Cross Society. After years of planning and praying and after months of watching and waiting, we have come at last to open this beautiful, long-awaited and much-needed facility. Thanks be to God!*
>
> *This building stands not only as a testimony to the public-spiritedness and generosity of all those who have contributed to its construction, but it also stands as a tribute to the dedication and hard work of the Red Cross staff and volunteers who for too long were forced to work under less than ideal conditions.*
>
> *The Red Cross has come a long way since it was established in The Bahamas a half century ago. It has broadened its scope, increased its range of services and modified its outreach*

approach with a view towards engendering an even greater level of participation and support from the community at large. Through all of this, the Society has guarded well its integrity and has engaged solely in the mission for which it was founded: alleviating human suffering while promoting the health and overall well-being of all Bahamians.

Whatever success has come to the Bahamas Red Cross Society can be attributed to the close ties and positive partnership that it has developed with the general public. Speaking of the general public, I realize that it is always a risky business to single out individuals and organizations when there have been countless contributions. Perhaps you will forgive me, however, if I run the risk of mentioning those donors who were especially benevolent to us with regard to this new facility.

Firstly, I must mention Mr Colin Wells. After our very first successful Family Island Red Cross fair several years ago Mr Wells suggested that if we could maintain the drive we could raise enough money to build a national headquarters for the Red Cross. The Red Cross executive committee agreed with this suggestion.

Secondly, with that behind us, we then looked around for a possible site on which to build such a building. Thereupon, past President, Mrs Rowena Eldon, past Director-General, Mrs Lottie Tynes and myself called upon the late Lady Eunice Oakes, explained our mission to her and she readily agreed to donate a site to the Red Cross for the purpose of locating its headquarters. That generous act on the part of Lady Oakes set the process in motion the culmination of which we are witnessing today. We are most grateful.

The factor which contributed most to the accumulation of funds which allowed the Red Cross to improve its services to the community at large and to put up a building was the Family Island fairs.

Thirdly, therefore, I must mention the warm and generous people in our Family Islands who went all out to make our fairs major social events, the hotel owners who donated our accommodation, the owners of airplanes who flew us, free of charge, from island to island and the bands that provided exciting music at our fairs.

> *On behalf of the Bahamas Red Cross Society, I would like to say thank you to all of you who have given their time, talent or money towards this facility. You are assured of our heartfelt appreciation. This new headquarters will undoubtedly bring relief and comfort to the staff, volunteers and clients of the Red Cross, and it will serve as a constant incentive for all of us to work even harder to promote the ideals of caring and sharing throughout The Bahamas.*
>
> *Madam President, I am delighted, indeed honoured to now declare this new and beautiful Red Cross National Headquarters officially open.*

Lady Pindling felt proud and grateful on that day. She said that she had not been ashamed to beg for the Red Cross because she was asking for the Red Cross, not herself.

> *I had no inhibitions about it. I just asked and people gave so much ... I was having dinner at Annabelle's in London one evening, taken there by Mr Edward St George, and Mr Peter De Savary was our guest. He said "I heard you are raising funds for the Red Cross, it's a worthy cause." I told him yes, would you like to contribute? He said "certainly" and wrote a cheque for $30,000.*
>
> *Then, on another occasion, I visited Cat Cay, a wealthy enclave near Bimini. That Saturday night we raised another $12,000 or so from the residents.*

The work of the Bahamas Red Cross was enhanced considerably after it moved into its new headquarters. There was space to store increased supplies and to assist more persons in the community.

Between 1985 and 1986:

> *Emergency supplies in the form of furniture, cooking utensils, bed linen, clothing and perishables were issued to persons in Abaco, Andros, Cat Island, Ragged Island, Eleuthera, Exuma and Long Island.*
>
> *The new auditorium at the J. F. Kennedy Drive headquarters enabled the association to offer training sessions to large numbers of people in the community. Ten courses were offered in basic First Aid, 16 in emergency First Aid and 12 in CPR (cardiopulmonary resuscitation). In the Family Islands eight courses were offered*

in basic First Aid and four in CPR, bringing a total number of people trained by the Bahamas Red Cross to 577. Nearly 9,000 hot meals were provided to 396 indigent persons throughout the community. Twenty-four homes were cleaned twice a week for a total of 650 cleaning sessions, some in the Family Islands.[13]

Another project in which the Red Cross was involved was the After School Mentoring Programme. About 40 children aged from 7 to 15 from the Farm Road Urban Renewal Project attended classes in English and Maths. Nurses from the Government Blue Hill Road Clinic gave information on health and cleanliness.

Lady Pindling was greatly praised at the Annual Red Cross Ball held on 24 January 2005. The tribute began by acknowledging the devastation of the horrendous Boxing Day earthquake and tsunamis in the Indian Ocean and the assistance of the International Red Cross and Red Crescent societies which came to the aid of the dying, the displaced and the devastated. The world called on the Red Cross because it knew of this group's legacy of relief in times of natural disaster and its care for the vulnerable in normal times. The tribute continued:[14]

And this very same spirit which drives the International Red Cross also animates our national Red Cross and the stellar contribution Lady Marguerite Pindling has made over the decades of the Red Cross movement.

Lady Pindling's contributions are built on the solid foundation of her vision for the development of the Bahamian people. She has helped foster national pride and self-help; personal and social development; and care for the poor and vulnerable. Through the graciousness of her personality and singular style she has cultivated the common good by bringing together people from diverse political, economic and social backgrounds. Her public duties were outward expressions of her private faith and character. She took seriously the biblical mandate to serve the least among us and expressed this in her personal commitment to all Bahamians irrespective of their social standing or background.

Along with her duties as a spouse, mother, friend, role model and wife of the Prime Minister, Lady Pindling involved herself enthusiastically in numerous philanthropic causes, including the Red Cross. She realized early on that good ideas had to be institutionalized. Accordingly she recognized the need to help broaden and deepen the development of the Red Cross fairs throughout The Bahamas and to help secure a permanent home for the organization.

And so she took the Red Cross movement to the people – literally. Along with other dedicated companions she took it from Grand Bahama to Governor's Harbour; from South Andros to South Eleuthera; from Matthew Town to Marsh Harbour; from Cat Island to Bimini and beyond. During these travels – which she calls a "labour of love" – she united the country around the value of service and instilled in our people a commitment to self-help.

These travels not only raised money, they also raised spirits. She insisted: "If the Red Cross Fair was good enough for people in Nassau then it was good enough for people in Nicoll's Town." In short she believed that every Bahamian should be connected to the Red Cross, but through the Red Cross she was also promoting Bahamian unity, volunteerism and compassion.

When the Red Cross outgrew Longley House on Dowdeswell Street, she spearheaded, along with the late Rowena Eldon, then Director-General, Lottie Tynes and others, a campaign to secure a new home for the group. Because of Lady Pindling's personal efforts Lady Oakes dedicated the land on which the present headquarters is located. Though the securing of this gift was one of her more significant accomplishments as chair of the Fund-raising Committee from 1976 to 1992, she also helped secure numerous other in-kind and financial gifts valued in the hundreds of thousands of dollars.

As current chair of the Fair Committee she continues to ensure that the movement has the support of Bahamian households and the House of Assembly; that people are talking around the kitchen table and the Cabinet table as to how they may support the Red Cross; that people at both Arawak Cay and Lyford Cay are a part of the Red Cross's legacy of compassion, care and community service.

We salute Lady Pindling for the very same reason she received the Henri Dunant Award, the highest honour the International Red Cross can bestow. We salute her because through her contributions thousands of people have been comforted and healed; through her contributions the Bahamian Red Cross will be sustained for generations to come; through her contributions she has been a *model of citizen-service; and through her contributions we have all been inspired to serve. Is this not the greatest service of all?*

When asked whether her success stemmed from political support, she replied: "No doubt about it and there were times persons would want to talk politics and I'd say, not on this trip, this is Red Cross business. They would want to know how my husband was doing and all that and of course you know, Mrs Tynes was a stickler for perfection – we'll have none of that."

Lady Pindling did not deny that politics were important. She in fact was very political and would have made an excellent Member of Parliament and Minister. Her involvement in politics will be the subject of the next chapter.

6
Lady Pindling and Politics I

In an address at a Ladies' Fellowship luncheon at Great Abaco Beach Hotel, Marsh Habour, Abaco, on 13 August 1992, Lady Pindling revealed that she has "the almost unique perspective of having been involved, in one fashion or another, in every election for the last 35 years." She continued: "I just missed the campaign for the general elections of 1956 which took place in June 1956. I had just been married a month before in May. I was so green then I didn't know what a general election was."

Her husband Lynden O. Pindling was elected in 1956 and she learnt quickly about politics. By 1962, the year of the next general election, she admits: "I was not green any more. I, along with Ms Ursula and Catherine Coakley and other ladies, vigorously campaigned for my husband and Mr Orville Turnquest [then a PLP] in the South Central District of Nassau ... I have campaigned in every general election since, including some by-elections, and in many constituencies and islands."

In the run-up to the 1992 elections, by the time she gave the speech, she had "already campaigned vigorously in Nassau, Freeport, Bimini, Inagua, Eleuthera and Andros".

Lady Pindling supported her husband, Lynden Pindling, both in Opposition and in Government. She was fiercely loyal to him "and anybody who got in the way was disciplined. If there was something I could do to stop them – I would." As Leader of the Opposition, after the coming into effect of the new Constitution in 1964, Lynden Pindling was asked to nominate two senators. Apparently, without consulting the National General Council or his parliamentary colleagues collectively, he chose Charles Rhodriquez, a firm supporter and financial backer of the PLP, and Clifford Darling, president of the powerful Taxi-Cab Union. According to Paul Adderley and Orville Turnquest, at a Christmas cocktail party held at the latter's home, Pindling announced his choices for the Senate seats. Turnquest stated that "all hell broke loose" and the party broke up shortly afterwards. Pindling had consulted some of the parliamentary group individually. Adderley stated that Pindling had promised him that he would appoint H. M. Taylor,[1] founder member of the PLP and its first Chairman.

Members of the parliamentary group, headed by Adderley and Turnquest, came to his home and confronted Pindling, demanding his resignation.

Lady Pindling "quickly ran to her bedroom and rang Arthur Foulkes at *The Bahamian Times* and he summoned Jeffrey Thompson who lived nearby and he came quickly". They were members of the National Council for Positive Action (NCPA) which included Arthur Foulkes, Warren Levarity, Sinclair Outten, Eugene Newry, Cadwell Armbrister and Jeffrey Thompson. Lady Pindling then left the room.

After speaking privately with Paul Adderley, Deputy Leader, Lynden Pindling acknowledged that he had acted against their wishes but asked for forgiveness, which was granted. Pindling promised to work closely with them in future.[2] Lady Pindling had acted in the best interest of her husband. By calling members of the NCPA, the situation was diffused – the attempted "Christmas Coup" as it was later labelled, had failed.[3]

Although Lynden Pindling never discussed Cabinet decisions with her, if Lady Pindling heard something she thought he should know, she would "put him on his guard so he would know how to deal with the situation". She admits:

> *He was my best friend and I was his best friend. We had political associates because of their being in Cabinet ... and their wives ... but I had no personal friends, none! That is why after we lost in 1992 I felt so alone. Being at the top was a very lonely life, but at least you knew who were your friends. The ordinary people were our friends. I was able to call up my women friends from the Women's Branch of the Party ... I could talk to them and they would talk to me and tell me what they heard ... so that I could tell the Leader. I did not feel inclined to call the wives of the Cabinet ministers ...*

Lady Pindling was upset by the reaction of some Cabinet ministers' wives when their husbands were moved from one ministry to another. She felt that they should have realized that is the way governments operate, "but they got upset because they figured it [the ministry] was theirs and felt they should not have been moved." She recalls that in 1972, when Sir Lynden shuffled his Cabinet and Arthur Hanna was removed from Home Affairs and Carl Francis from Finance, Beryl Hanna and Christine Francis were very hostile and cold towards her: "They showed it when we went to the Constitutional Conference in 1972 ... I felt it – it was like a knife cutting through me – I felt isolated." But she realized that: "There are no friends in this business and as the saying goes, uneasy lies the head that wears the crown; I would not sit around with my head buried in the sand because I had to defend and protect him in whichever way I was able to. I tried to do that to the best that I could."

Although Lady Pindling had no university degrees, she had much common sense and intuition. She states: "I knew when they were plotting and planning because your common sense would tell you. You could feel it and sense it and you didn't just sit there and allow it to happen. You got out there and gathered your forces and once I had my forces together we went with him. The people saw what was happening and they wanted him to do what he did. As I look back now, I believe the saying, that leaders are not made; they are born."

In a moving farewell speech to the Bahamian Parliament, Sir Lynden Pindling expressed his regret at not having shielded Lady Pindling and the children from all the "slings and arrows"[4] of the outer world. She acknowledges that "he tried his best to protect us". However, she undertook to protect him and give him all the support at home along with the support of the people. "The people were with us – all the time – all the way so whenever I moved, people were there with me."

Progressive Liberal Party women were most supportive of Sir Lynden and Lady Pindling. She admits that her fierce loyalty probably caused her to "do some things for which she was criticized". Former Attorney General and Minister of Foreign Affairs, the Honourable Paul L. Adderley, told her once that she "was the only wife he knew that liked to get mixed up in politics". She retorted: "I'm sorry if you feel that way, but I have a husband and I have to watch his back." Sir Lynden always had the support of PLP women and that gave Lady Pindling confidence that he would not be upset or unseated. Moreover, the women raised funds for travel in the early days. She relates: "Our husbands had other things to do so the women would go out and encourage the women. I didn't miss a beat, I went everywhere … and came to know so many people."

Marguerite Pindling campaigned on the Out (Family) Islands after three Cat Island women were imprisoned in 1964 over a land issue in favour of a company owned by one of the United Bahamian Party's Members of Parliament, Mr Harold G. Christie. During the previous year, Cat Island Farms Company Limited, owned by Christie, submitted an application, which was granted to the Supreme Court, to cease cultivating the land "pending a final decision to the title to the land".[5] The Court's order was defied by about 25 Cat Island farmers, and three Cat Island women were imprisoned for between 21 and 28 days for contempt of court and were "refused leave to appeal to the Privy Council".[6] At that time there was no court of appeal in The Bahamas. It was established in 1965. Milo Butler, an early fiery freedom fighter, and then a member of the PLP, led a deputation of farmers to Government House and during a "solemn" moment in the House of Assembly (the day after Sir George Robert died), shouted: "Three negro women have been sent to gaol and nobody cares a damn about them."[7]

Marguerite Pindling and Beryl Hanna spent eight days in Old Bight, Cat Island, sleeping in Lazarus Dawkins's family home on a grass bed. It was rough, especially for Mrs Hanna. There was no electricity or running water or inside toilets, and they had to use an outside toilet or potty. Despite the hardships, Dame Marguerite says: "We thoroughly enjoyed our stay in Old Bight. There was a lady named Gilena Wells who was a tower of strength. She was so proud and full of fight; she loved her party and wanted to see justice brought for her women. Of course Mr H. G. Christie took their land and put them in jail. There was also a lady, Ms Adelaide Armbrister, who went to prison for their own land."

Dame Marguerite remembers cooking for PLP lawyers including Cecil Wallace Whitfield and Arthur Hanna while they worked on the case. She says: "There were a lot of things we had to do. We didn't win the government in 1962 as expected and remained in Opposition for five more years. I was there in the trenches, that is why I don't mind what is said about me. What I am, who I am, I've earned my place, I worked for it. I didn't sit down. I worked when we were in Opposition and I worked even harder when we became the Government."

Lady Pindling's role in keeping her husband in power was significant. She apprised him of things she had heard and also kept in touch with the "fellows" for details of problems he was encountering. People also used her as a go-between – a way to get to Lynden Pindling. "The people used to come to me with a lot of things – I want you to tell my leader so and so is the case, and go to such and such a person, or look out for what they're planning for him for this is what we heard." There was a network. Very often it came from the women who were strongly supportive. She waited for the right moment to intervene on their behalf if she thought it was a valid matter. Lynden Pindling would contact the person and encouraged his wife also to follow up on important issues. She marvelled that her husband remembered to call or write and saw to it that she did the same thing. He was particular about this and it made people "feel appreciated". The Pindlings also made sure to thank people who would have helped them. While her husband was in office, she gave gifts at Christmas to many people, although it was expensive. It was their way of saying "thank you".

Lady Pindling had a fighting spirit and faced criticisms undaunted. She recalls that she felt that the more educated members of the PLP looked down on her, and some made remarks such as: "If you want to fry conch fritters and fry fish go see Marguerite – you want a letter typed, you could bring it to me." She retorted, "I said that's alright – frying conch fritters and frying fish took them straight to Buckingham Palace and I had helped to pave the way for them to get there." She continued "It was a struggle of

59. Mrs Pindling visits the House of Commons, London, in the early 1970s

60. Mrs Pindling at the launching of the SS *Freeport* in 1968

61. Marguerite Pindling and Father William Thompson greeting Mr Arthur Hanna, Deputy Prime Minister, after attending a church service

62. Mrs Pindling on her way to the House of Assembly, late 1960s

63. Mrs Pindling hosts a ladies' luncheon at a PLP Convention, late 1960s/early 1970s

64. Lady Darling, Dame Doris Johnson and Mrs Pindling in the early 1970s. *Photo: Vincent D. Vaughan*

65. Signing of the Panama Canal Treaty, 1977

66. The Pindlings with Ernest Strachan, Chief of Protocol in the 1970s, heading to a conference

67. Mrs Pindling attends a banquet of the Business and Professional Women's Association. From left: Nazla Dane, Lady Butler, Marguerite Pindling and Barbara Pierre

68. Mizpah Tertullien, Lynden Pindling, Lady Butler and Sir Milo Butler at a Testimonial Banquet by the Women's Branch of the PLP, February 1977. *Photo: Bruce Delancey*

69. Mrs Pindling examines a gift of a bottle of perfume from the women delegates at a PLP convention; Dame Doris Johnson in the background.
Photo: Howard Glass, Bahamas News Bureau

70. The Pindlings at the White House with President Carter, Mrs Carter, Mr Ford and Lady Bird Johnson, 1977

71. Mrs Angie Brookes, Secretary General at the United Nations, meets the Pindlings on a visit to Nassau

72. Mrs Marguerite Pindling and Mrs Charmaine Johnson

73. Mr and Mrs Pindling on the way to the palace to celebrate the Queen's Silver Jubilee in 1977

74. Mrs Marguerite Pindling and Mrs Carlton Francis, wife of the Minister of Education.
Photo: Frederic Maura, Bahamas News Bureau

75. The Pindlings enjoy a light moment at the Family Island Regatta, George Town, Exuma, at the Crow's Nest

76. The Pindlings with methodist minister, Rev. Edwin Taylor and Mrs Taylor.

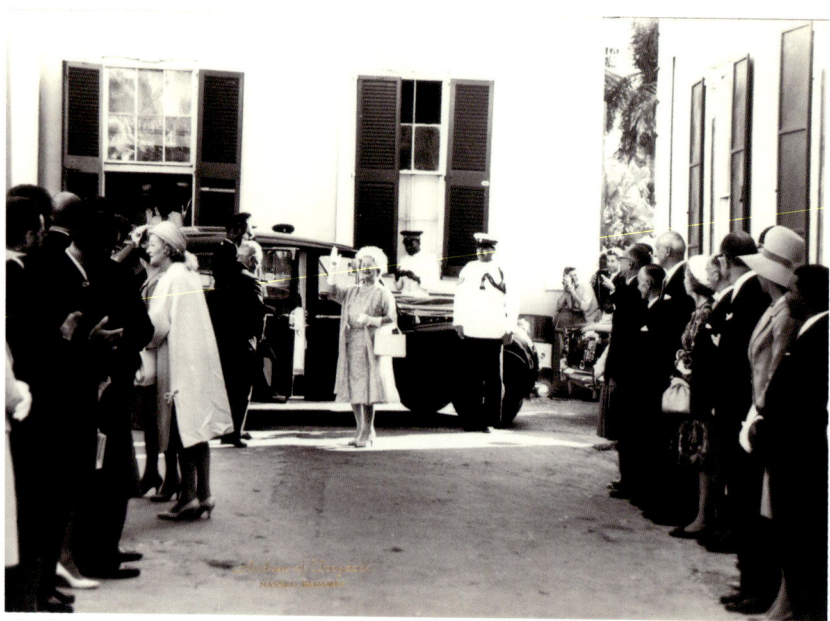

77. HM Queen Elizabeth the Queen Mother stops in Nassau in the mid- to late 1960s on her way to Kingston, Jamaica; the Pindlings are seen in the foreground, far right. *Photo: Toogoods*

78. Her Majesty the Queen speaks at a rally in 1977 at Clifford Park while the Duke of Edinburgh, the Prime Minister and Mrs Pindling, and Mrs Arthur Hanna look on. *Photo: Frederic Maura, Bahamas News Bureau*

79. The Pindlings' first official function at the Lyford Cay Club in the late 1960s, with Mrs Penny Dauphinot and Mr Clarence Dauphinot

80. Mrs Lynden Pindling, Mrs Leslie Shelton, wife of the US Ambassador and Lady Gray at a Christmas tableau outside the House of Assembly.

81. Lady Pindling with Defence Force officers in the early 1980s

82. Marguerite Pindling, Lynden Pindling and Vernice Moultrie Cooper at Happy People Marina in Staniel Cay, Exuma, 1970s

83. Lady Pindling speaking at the opening of Casurinas, West Bay Street, in the late 1980s

84. Mrs Pindling and Lady Cumming-Bruce inspecting the Girl Guides in Matthew Town, Inagua, late 1970s

85 The Pindlings with Mr and Mrs Edward Seaga, Prime Minister of Jamaica at CHOGM, 1975, in Jamaica

86. Sir Milo Butler, Governor-General, HM the Queen, Mr Lynden Pindling, Lady Butler, HRH Prince Philip and Mrs Pindling, about 1977

87. Marguerite Pindling, L. B. Johnson, Lynden Pindling and the Hon. Paul Adderley, Minister of Foreign Affairs, at the United Nations in July 1973, when The Bahamas became a member of the United Nations

88. The Pindlings with Prince Charles at Government House in July 1973 during Independence celebrations

89. Sir Lynden and Lady Pindling with Jamaican President Edward Seaga at The Bahamas Independence Celebrations in 1973

90. Mohammed Ali, his wife and friends visit the Pindlings at their residence, Long Bay, in the early 1980s. *Photo: Howard Glass*

91. The Prime Minister and Lady Pindling with Catholic Archbishop Lawrence Burke and Sir Kendal and Lady Isaacs.

92. Mrs Marguerite Pindling dancing with Winston V. Saunders, chairman of the Dundas Centre for the Performing Arts

93. Mrs Pindling – a portrait by Vincent D. Vaughan, photographer, in 1980

94 Obi Pindling's Call to the Bar, Supreme Court, Nassau, 1980

95. Mrs Pindling with the Red Cross Youth Group at the Red Cross Fair, Government House Grounds

96. Mrs Pindling drawing a raffle ticket for the Crippled Children's Fund; also pictured are Carlton Williams and Shirley Oakes Butler, Chair of the comittee.
Photo: Wendell Cleare, Bahamas Tourist News Bureau

97. Mrs Pindling offering a piece of cake to a student at the Stapledon School for the Mentally Retarded

98. Mrs Pindling attends the opening of the Garden Clubs of Nassau; from left: Mrs Grace Isaacs, Lady Cumming-Bruce, Mrs Pindling, (unidentified), and Mrs Zoe Maynard.
Photo: Lorenzo Lockhart, Bahamas Tourist News Bureau

99. Mr Billy Dee Williams and Mrs Marguerite Pindling at the official opening of a Red Cross Fair in Government House grounds in the early 1980s. *Photo: Vincent D. Vaughan*

100. Mrs Pindling, co-chair of the Red Cross Fair committee, with committee members in Freeport, Grand Bahama, mid-1970s

101. Members of the Red Cross Raffle Committee with the car which was raffled. *Photo: Andrew Aitken Photography*

102. Mrs Pindling (third from right) with children from Red Bay, Andros, after they completed a one-day tour of Nassau. The children had lunch with Mrs Pindling at McDonalds, 10 June 1980. *Photo: E. Bruce Delancey.*

103. Burning of the Mortgage, Children's Emergency Hostel. Photo: *E. Bruce Delancey.*

104. Mrs Pindling accepts vegetables raised in the garden of the Children's Emergency Hostel, 26 January 1974. *Photo: Howard Glass.*

105. The Red Cross Fair committee visits Spanish Wells; Mrs Rowena Eldon, President of the Bahamas Red Cross Committee, is on the left, and Mrs Pindling far right

106. Mrs Pindling sells raffle tickets for the Bahamas Association for the Mentally Retarded.
Photo: Vincent D. Vaughan

107. Mrs Pindling making cash donations to various charities

108. Mrs Pindling gives a rousing speech at a PLP women's luncheon in the late 1970s.
Photo: Raymond A. Bethel

109. Lady Pindling speaking at a pre-election fellowship luncheon on 26 July 1992

110. Mr and Mrs Lynden Pindling on the way to the House of Assembly in the 1980s

111. The Pindlings (Sir Lynden was then Leader of the Opposition), being presented to HM the Queen on an official visit in 1993; the Rt Hon. Hubert A. Ingraham, Prime Minister, is standing to the right of the Queen

112. Lady Pindling with Canadian Prime Minister, Brian Mulroney and Mrs Mulroney. CHOGM, Nassau, 1985.

113. The Pindlings with the Prime Minister of Lesotho

114. The Pindlings with the Prime Minister of the Maldives and his wife

115. The Pindlings chat with Mr and Mrs Edward Seaga

116. Guests including Roman Catholic Bishop Burke, Joyce and Telford Georges, Robert Mugabe, President of Zimbabwe, and Sally Mugabe

117. Sir Lynden greets Rajiv Ghandi and Mrs Ghandi

118. HM Queen Elizabeth II greets Lady Pindling before the Command Performance of the folk opera *Sammy Swain* by Clement Bethel; CHOGM, Nassau, 1985

119. Lady Pindling and Sir Lynden with Sir John and Lady Compton of St Lucia

120. Lady Pindling, Sir Lynden and Kenneth Kaunda, President of Zambia, at the Balmoral Beach Hotel

121. Lady Pindling arrives at Government House, Nassau, to dine with HM Queen Elizabeth II, March 1993

the ordinary black people. Those same 'common' people you see out there paved the way and made it possible for them to feel so important. I don't want us to ever forget it was the people who put us there ... he was a people's person and that is why Sir Lynden is so loved – even after death."

Disloyalty was something Lady Pindling could not tolerate. She recalls that after the PLP's defeat in 1992, a "particular fellow came to our home and said, 'Your husband caused us to lose.' I said, 'If you don't get out of my house ... All the times Sir Lynden was campaigning for you, we won. This time he didn't ... he felt that the candidates were not deserving.'" Contrary to what others expressed, she clung to that belief. There were certain Cabinet ministers about whom she had reservations. She admitted that that "Loftus Roker ... was never Lynden's friend." In fact she doubted that he was anybody's friend. He shared an office with them in the Sassoon Building on Shirley Street. She got to know him and confesses that "He was a nice person mind you, but he was one of those that if you were his friend, you could not be a friend to anyone else." She recalls that Clement Maynard, on a visit to their office to see Loftus Roker, had a conversation with her and for some reason, she cannot remember why, he told her, "You need to go back to school." She never forgot those words.

She admired the loyalty and strength of Cabinet minister Jeffrey Thompson's wife, Merlene Thompson. Mrs Thompson sat in the House of Assembly until the early hours of the morning during the vote of no confidence in 1970 brought by Randol Fawkes against Lynden Pindling. She sent her husband a note: " 'I will not leave here until you speak and when you speak, you will speak in support of Pindling.' He was the last member to speak and that was at 3 a.m. ... She was another tough wife."

During the 1969 Convention, Pindling had a confrontation with his Minister of Education, Cecil Wallace-Whitfield, and demanded his resignation, requesting that it be on his desk by the following morning. Lynden Pindling called his wife at about 10 a.m. and said, "Honey, the fellows asked me to reconsider Cecil's resignation." She was adamantly against it and said, "But you can't do that." He said that for the sake of unity in the Party, "I have to withdraw my remarks." Lady Pindling was the quintessential politician. She never thought twice of getting rid of anyone who was "blocking progress". She actually liked Wallace-Whitfield: "He had a heart of gold and fire in his belly ... he was a nice fellow though."

At the PLP's convention in October 1970 Lynden Pindling, in the face of the rumour that there was a plot to overthrow him, stated in his opening speech that there were some in the Party who "have become overcome with envy and consumed with jealousy; and some have been stung by the serpent of greed. We have become too concerned with those who make ministers and who make Prime Ministers and have become too unconcerned with those who make representatives. Let us not fool ourselves as to where the ultimate power lies. It does not rest with me. It rests with the people."[8] He then uttered the now famous words to his critics: "If you can't fish, cut bait, if you can't cut bait, get the hell out of the boat."[9]

Cecil Wallace-Whitfield, who delivered the Convention's keynote address, criticized the "creeping totalitarianism within the party" and ended by resigning from the Cabinet, quoting Martin Luther King's well-known words, "Free, free at last, my soul is free at last." Seven other PLP rebels, Curtis Macmillan, Arthur Foulkes, Warren Levarity, Maurice Moore, Elwood Donaldson, James Shepherd and George Thompson followed Whitfield, voting against Pindling on the no confidence vote, and eventually formed the Free National Movement.

Earlier in 1968 Rev. Uriah McPhee, who represented Shirlea, died. The PLP then had a majority of one. In 1967 the PLP and UBP were tied with 18 seats each. Alvin Braynen, an Independent, had agreed to become the Speaker, and Sir Randol of the Labour Party was made Minister of Labour in a PLP administration. What was Premier Pindling to do? Should he call a by- or general election? He asked his wife for her opinion. Realizing that the people were "still in the 1967 mood", she agreed that he should go for the general election.

Mrs Pindling continued campaigning side by side with her husband and during the early 1970s it was rumoured that she wished to run for a seat in the House of Assembly. This turned out to be untrue. A stronger rumour appeared in the *Nassau Guardian* of 12 May 1987, when it was stated that the "National General Council of the PLP in a special session ratified Lady Pindling, wife of the Prime Minister Sir Lynden as the party's candidate in Central Andros (Mangrove Cay constituency) and approved Darrell E. Rolle, present Member of Parliament for Mangrove Cay, as the standard bearer in Nicholls Town (North Andros) in the upcoming General Election."[10]

Apparently, the PLP leaders in Mangrove Cay were willing to "yield" Mr Rolle only if the Prime Minister or Lady Pindling offered to run in Mangrove Cay. The *Nassau Guardian* also reported that the Prime Minister had informed leaders in the Fresh Creek School Room that "it was going to be Lady Pindling". Lady Pindling denied these assertions – they were only rumours. She added that the time she seriously thought of running was in 1967 and only in the event that her husband could not nominate as he was out of the country on Party business.

Lady Pindling's speeches in the political context sometimes proved controversial. In her remarks to the Women's Regional Branches of the Progressive Liberal Party on 16 June 1983, she spoke of the role of women and the important contribution they had made in The Bahamas. She stated that "the majority of women in this country have for the past 16 years stood so idly and resolutely behind our great Progressive Liberal Party" but she urged them not to take this support for granted. It was "our responsibility to protect our stake". She then commented on how "heartening and encouraging" it was to see that four Regional Women's Branches were formed. "It signalled that we were alive and kicking ... but are we alive and kicking? Or are we just existing?" She continued:

> *If we PLP women are alive and kicking what is our position on Leonard Archer? Have we so little interest in our children's education that we remain silent and allow any teacher to let his students out of school any hour of the school day to do what they want? Do we think that a Senior High School Principal does not know that a school child cannot present a petition to Parliament? That it must be given to a Member of Parliament? That if a student wished to take a petition to a Member of Parliament, he could take it after school hours? Have we fallen asleep? Do we not care?*

The speech was directed at A. Leonard Archer, then President of the Bahamas Union of Teachers. The Bahamas Union of Teachers (BUT), according to A. Leonard Archer, was perhaps the "most dynamic union in the 1970s and came to be seen as a union in opposition to the Government". The 1970s were difficult years, what with high inflation and the oil shock of 1974. The BUT, besides fighting for improved conditions and pay for its members, was also concerned about the high rate of unemployment and prospects for the students when they graduated.

Lady Pindling's speech was prompted by the demonstration of R. M. Bailey Senior High School students on Bay Street in February 1983. Apparently, the student body of R. M. Bailey had asked their principal, Mr A. Leonard Archer, if they could present a petition to Parliament about the condition of schools and the job market in The Bahamas. Mr Archer thought that such actions by the children were helping to develop a sense of civic responsibility and action, and he gave the student council permission to go during one of their lunch breaks. However, the student council subsequently met with the student body and some of the students wished to join the student council. About one hundred students proceeded to Parliament Square and presented the petition to the Clerk of the House of Assembly. One student, interviewed by the Broadcasting Corporation of The Bahamas (ZNS), stated that Mr A. Leonard Archer had given them all permission, while in fact he had meant only the student council.[11]

Part of this speech was broadcast on ZNS radio, and a letter written by Lady Pindling asking Leonard Archer if he was Communist, and hinting that she would make public sensitive and personal information about him, appeared in the Press. The BUT took exception to the remarks in her speech and letter referring to A. Leonard Archer, president of the Union. In a statement the BUT urged the Prime Minister's wife "to leave matters of this nature to those who know something about them".[12] It sarcastically commented that "Apparently Lady Pindling thinks that since she has been given a colonial title, she is capable of commenting on matters of this nature." It continued:

> Since Lady Pindling wishes to speak on national issues, we suggest she champion young people's causes for jobs when they leave school; she should speak out on the lack of day care facilities for working women; the problem of young girls being exploited by older men; problems of housing, and drug use and abuse in our society; we doubt that Lady Pindling has the courage to address these issues as anything said would be an indictment against the Government. She has however surprised us by speaking out of ills in our society which in large part are due mainly to governmental neglect that people have suffered.[13]

Leonard Archer also wrote, "I can live with my past, can you live with yours?" and denied having encouraged students to demonstrate and petition parliamentarians.

Lady Pindling's remarks about Leonard Archer, activist leader of the Bahamas Union of Teachers and critic of the PLP Government, also stirred the Trade Union Congress leaders to warn that it intended to notify the International Labour Organization and the International Confederation of Free Trade Unions of the "threat to Mr Archer and the threat to trade unionism in general in the Bahamas."[14] The article alluded to the rumour that the Ministry of Education planned to discipline and fire Mr Archer because of the political statement made. In fact, Mr Archer was put into early retirement by the Ministry.

Two months later on 20 August 1983, Lady Pindling, while addressing the first Women's Convention of the PLP at the South Ocean Beach Hotel, commented: "In the working of ... democracy we also saw what was meant by the old saying that he who rides the back of a tiger is likely to wind up inside its belly. Mr Leonard Archer, who for years had used and misused teachers and children for his own purposes, was finally forced to part company with the Ministry of Education."

In fact, because of growing disenchantment with the PLP Government the speech was poignantly political. She urged women to get "more involved … and stay involved". She continued:

> *This is not the time to allow ourselves to be lulled into a false sense of security. We must not allow ourselves to be placated by the progress we have achieved, for today, in this country, the political enemies are going about as roaring lions seeking whom they may devour.*
>
> *Former United States President Theodore Roosevelt once felt: "We cannot afford to blind ourselves to the actual conflict which faces us today. The issue is joined: we must fight or fail." Indeed we must fight or fail.*
>
> *Gone are the days when we had to fight only during the election time; those days are gone! There are forces amongst us that are preaching strange political doctrines, and they are trying their best to poison the minds of our children with their anti-everything gospel. The FNM is telling the country, and young people in particular, that it's okay to break the law of the land as long as their actions are aimed against the Government. The Vanguard Party is telling our children that they can do whatever they want to do as long as it embarrasses the Government. Others still are content to use little, innocent children to make the Government look bad.*
>
> *I say that we have reached the crossroads. Our children's welfare and future are at stake. Which will it be? An era of political poison and treachery by our foes, or an era of law, order and discipline under the PLP? I ask: which will it be? An era by the PLP? Which will it be? An era of despair brought about by the detractors of progress, or an era of hope brought about by the party of progress?*
>
> *I have heard that our opponents intend to light a fire under the PLP. What they ought to realize by now is that when the heat is up, the quality of the metal is exposed. We've been in hot kitchens before. We will fight, and we will not fail!*
>
> *Needless to say, Madam Chairman, we of this great party, the people's party, we who are the guardians of the people's trust must fight a different kind of fight. While those who oppose us fight with doubt, we must fight with hope; while they fight with words*

of poison, we must fight with words of reason; while they fight with the welfare of our children, we must fight for the future of our children; while they fight with The Tribune, we must fight with our togetherness; while they fight by their inaction, we must fight with our positive, constructive action. That's the way we will fight, and that is why we will not fail.

Madam Chairman, ladies and gentlemen, we have a wonderful country. Notwithstanding the social problems and the fears generated by the lawless in our society, we still have a good society in which law and order are respected by almost all our citizens. In our country we have seen to it that the system is preserved whereby justice is available to all.

Today we Bahamians are sovereign and free. We are free to be responsible or irresponsible; free to be nation makers or duty shirkers; free to be character builders or character breakers; free to be a participator or a spectator; free to get involved or sit on the fence; free to neglect our children or to save them. Yes, we are a free people, but freedom, positive, productive and progressive freedom, isn't always free. True freedom requires participation, consolidation, unification and dedication. We in this great party still have a destiny to create, thus we must fight vigorously against those who will enslave us with their foreign doctrines and lawless ways. We must vigorously fight against those who will poison the minds of our children by their anti-everything antics and alien doctrines of disrespect for authority.

Let us go forth from this convention as servants of the country, as bearers of the truth, as party stalwarts all. Let us offer common-sense remedies resting on historical understanding. Let us study our past errors without alleging meanness and motive. Let us seek to unite rather than to destroy.

As PLP women we must not fail in our never-ending quest to improve this nation. We must hold sacred our tradition of loyalty and morality. We must guard against destructive, false criticism and apathy. We must never surrender to purveyors of doubt and perpetrators of evil. I fully believe that divine providence has provided us with an opportunity to save and serve our country. If we leave this convention dedicated to that purpose, our duty as PLP women will have been nobly done.

Madam Chairman, together, let us fight, not fail.

Perhaps the most controversial speech that Lady Pindling ever delivered was just prior to the 1987 election. During the campaign in June 1987 in a hotly contested election – the FNM was gaining in popularity – Lady Pindling, two weeks before polling day, spoke to a crowd of about 2,000 PLP supporters. The *Nassau Guardian* reported under a headline of "Bahamians owe me, says Lady Pindling":

> Making a rare appearance on a public platform, Lady Pindling, wife of Prime Minister Pindling, told PLP supporters in Elizabeth Estates on Tuesday evening [2 June 1987] that the Prime Minister had given 31 years of his life to the Bahamian country and its people and as his wife, she also has given time to the people of The Bahamas. Therefore the Bahamian people owed her and could repay her on June 19th.

The article continued:

> Addressing hundreds on the basketball court at Elizabeth Estates, Lady Pindling said: "I am the wife of the man, and I want you to know that my man has given his life to serve you and your country. June 8th will make it 31 years since he was elected to the House of Assembly. I have also given 31 years to you, my people of this country, and you owe me something; you owe me a husband, you owe me a father, you owe me a son to his parents, and I want you to know, come hell or high water, on the 19th day of this month, you should pay up."[15]

At this point, intrigued and surprised by Lady Pindling's spontaneous remarks, numerous persons who had been sitting in their cars came to the ball court in spite of the rain and "refused to move". Lady Pindling continued:

> "On election day, you give me my birthday present, because my birthday is on June 26th ... just like you gave me Rose [PLP candidate Matthew Rose who was elected in a by-election for St Barnabas]. And let us continue on the good foot we started since 1967. Since today I had some people call me to tell me about my husband but I want all of you tomorrow morning when you look in the mirror to look at your faces. I want you to remember that the face you see in the mirror is the face of Lynden Pindling and the PLP because what you're enjoying today is Pindling and the PLP. I don't care what the FNM say, because they are an ungrateful bunch, and God does not like

ingratitude, because what you are, what they are, is because of this great Progressive Liberal Party of ours."[16]

This speech caused quite a stir. Lady Pindling said that she was completely misunderstood. She only wished to celebrate her birthday with another PLP victory. However, seven days later several letters containing scathing criticism of Lady Pindling's remarks appeared. A person who signed him/herself as "A First Time Voter" retorted that "neither I nor the Bahamian people owes her a dime ... Everything you and your husband did for this country was your DUTY."[17] The writer continued the criticism by saying that her place was not on the "platform" but in the "front seat".

Another critical letter was written by Mr Keod Smith, who later joined the PLP and was elected as a Member of the House of Assembly for Mount Moriah in 2002 under Perry Christie's leadership. Mr Smith stated that while Sir Lynden had given his time and efforts to public life, he had also reaped "financial and social benefits for himself, Lady Pindling, their children and parents". He demanded an apology and that Lady Pindling "rescind her 'ridiculous claim on the Bahamian people'".[18]

The Free National Movement was also critical of Lady Pindling's speech and published a press release on 9 June 1987 in *The Tribune* under the by-line "Bahamians owe Lady P. nothing". It reminded Lady Pindling that parliamentarians and ministers are paid "by the people for their services", that those who hold political office "have the right to resign office when they no longer wish to serve" and that Lady Pindling had assumed the role of First Lady of the country "which rightly belongs to the wife of the Governor-General, the Head of State". The press release continued: "It is the Pindlings who owe the Bahamian people" and asked for an "explanation for the huge sums of money that were found in their bank accounts ... and the luxurious life style that she and her husband have pursued over the last 20 years."[19]

Journalist Basil Smith, who later became an executive in the Bahamas Ministry of Tourism and director of Jamaica's Ministry of Tourism, commented on the incident in the *Bahamian Review* of August 1987: "In one of the more controversial highlights of the last election campaign ... Lady Pindling, who had traditionally eschewed the cut and thrust of the political fray, went public with the frustration she felt as a wife and member of his family for the years of sacrifice which he [Sir Lynden] had invested in his career as leader of the modern Bahamas."

He continued that although Lady Pindling's comments may have been "resented, misunderstood or misinterpreted in some quarters, they struck a responsive cord in that area of Bahamian society where more voters were concentrated than anywhere else: the single family households headed by women; the working class which has looked to Sir Lynden for economic and social advancement and progress for two decades."[20]

In fact, Lady Pindling "did get the birthday present which she had asked for in the emotional heat ... of the political rally – an unprecedented, for the entire region, fifth term in office [for Lynden Pindling] as a democratically elected leader."[21]

7
Lady Pindling and Politics II

The early 1980s were difficult years for The Bahamas and the Government headed by Sir Lynden Pindling. Drug-trafficking from South America and the Caribbean through Bahamian waters to the United States, the main consumer market, was evident from the late 1960s, then escalated and by 1983 had reached "staggering proportions".[1] Bahamians stood accused of profiting from a clandestine business which echoed its opportunistic involvement historically with piracy, wrecking, blockade-running and rum-running.

Although the Police Marine Division (set up in 1974) and later the Royal Bahamas Defence Force were aware from the mid- to late 1970s of the seriousness of drug-trafficking through The Bahamas and seizures were made, they were no match for the powerful cartels which established networks covering the entire Bahamian archipelago for their nefarious trade. There was intermittent cooperation between the United States and Bahamian authorities but American agencies often acted without the knowledge of the Bahamian authorities, employing secret agents using subversive methods in their quest to catch drug smugglers. As the drug-running increased and Bahamians became involved, drugs used as payment began to be sold to Bahamians. The drug-smuggling foreigners also brought in guns, and crime levels rose.

US and Bahamian relations deteriorated after an expose of the drug-trafficking in The Bahamas in the *Wall Street Journal* in 1982. But it reached its lowest ebb in September 1983, when the NBC in a news programme "alleged that Prime Minister Pindling was involved in widespread drug corruption". To add to the shocking news a series of articles in the *Miami Herald* between 23 September and 10 October 1983 entitled "A Nation for Sale: Corruption in The Bahamas" appeared. These "revealed an abortive 'sting' operation carried out by US agents aiming to entrap a Bahamian Cabinet Minister."[2]

Bahamians were shocked and the Government outraged. Sir Lynden Pindling defended himself by appearing on NBC television denying the charges. He cut his interview short and threatened to sue the network for defamation. The case against the "ambushed" Cabinet minister was dropped. Bahamian sovereignty came to the fore and influenced the anti-American stance of the Bahamian Government over the invasion of Grenada which occurred just a month after the NBC and *Miami Herald* bombshells. The Opposition FNM made the most of these accusations and ensured that copies of the newspaper articles were circulated and extracts published in two of the local papers – *The Tribune* and *Guardian*. It also called for Prime Minister Pindling's resignation.

Lady Pindling remembers the pain she felt when accusations were made against her husband by NBC's Brian Ross. She recalls: "I could remember that evening ... Sir Lynden had just walked into the house and Obi and I were watching the news because we had heard that something was coming on ... this man [Brian Ross] was making these accusations against him saying that he was being paid $100,000 a year to turn a blind eye."

They were all shocked. Their son Obi was particularly upset – he "gripped his stomach and started rocking in the chair and said: 'What is this? Where did this come from?' Everybody's mouths dropped open because it was so ridiculous and my husband just stood staring – $100,000 a year to look the other way."

According to Michael Craton, Sir Lynden was "ambushed" by Brian Ross when he appeared on NBC television. He had been told roughly what would be asked. However, Jane Pauley, who interviewed him (with Brian Ross in the background) "departed completely from the script, presented the allegations as if they were already proven facts"; the information had been obtained from various sources not known to others as yet. Sir Lynden was justifiably angry and "came across as flustered, overly defensive and evasive". He stated that they could not expect him to answer charges as he did not know who made them, why they were made and where they had come from.[3]

Lady Pindling was especially upset for her children. Her son Leslie at the time was working in a hotel in Amsterdam. While watching television, he saw his father's image on the screen and heard all these derogatory remarks about him – harbouring drug lords in The Bahamas and having been paid off. He said he was stunned and was fortunate that no one knew he was a Pindling. They only knew him as Leslie. He said he went to the bathroom and wept because of the comments about his father.

The Pindlings' two daughters, Michelle and Monique, were in school in London. Dame Marguerite states: "I was shocked to see them on television leaving their flat to go to school. Cameras were following my children because of who they were – because of the untruth." Apparently the British press had found out where Michelle and Monique lived. She admits that "I hurt to this day because they had no proof of all the accusations that were levied against my husband. In fact, they proved nothing." At the end of

November 1983, Prime Minister Pindling called a Commission of Inquiry "to inquire into the illegal use of The Bahamas for the transshipment of dangerous drugs destined for the United States of America".

The Commission comprised a former Chief Justice, Sir James Smith, Bahamian Bishop of Barbados Drexel Gomez (later Bishop of The Bahamas and The Turks and Caicos and Archbishop of The West Indies), a senior officer of the Royal Canadian Mounted Police, Edwin Willis, and Chief Investigator Robert Ellicott QC, former Attorney General of Australia. The Commission's mandate was to examine drug transshipment, the involvement in drug-running of ministers, Members of Parliament and civil servants, the adequacy of Bahamian law-enforcement of penalties, and relations with US enforcement agencies.[4]

Convened on 7 December 1983, the Commission sat for 146 days which included 95 days of public testimony, 40 days of closed sessions in Nassau and 11 days of closed sessions in Miami. The Commission of Inquiry revealed that drugs posed one of the most serious social problems. Drug corruption pervaded every level of society and government. Even more problematic, the drugs themselves had become so readily available and relatively cheap in the islands that a large number of Bahamians, many of them young, were addicted, thus attracting the wrong type of visitor to the islands. Drug-related profits distorted the economy, and the easy and ill-gotten wealth upset the material and moral values of Bahamians.[5]

Sir Lynden, while he was convinced that the United States Government did much to discredit his Government by sending in false witnesses and double-agents, acknowledged: "That does not detract from the fact that it, the smuggling of drugs, was widespread, from Abaco to Inagua. Pervasive. All through." He admitted that his Government was aware of drug-running but "did not have the capacity to do everything on our own". Americans knew this and wished to blame the Bahamian Government for it "as if it were our idea. As if we instigated it. As if we encouraged it. And as if we are doing nothing about it. And all the time the real drug lords were building skyscrapers in Miami."[6]

But the drug problem was real and as Michael Craton said, "to an extent the government could properly be held responsible for it. But it was not criminally liable."[7] In fact very few persons were proved guilty of actual wrongdoing.

Sir Lynden was personally cleared of any wrongdoing. However, a rigorous scrutiny of his finances showed that Pindling had received approximately five times his official salary between 1977 and 1983. Two of the three members of the Commission concluded that it could not be proved that any of the monies were drug related. Bishop Drexel Gomez, however, stated in his minority report:

> It is certainly feasible that all of these payments could have been made from non-drug related sources. But in my opinion, the circumstances raised great suspicions and I find it impossible to say that the payments were all non-drug related. Some could have been but ... it certainly cannot be contested that the Prime Minister did not exercise sufficient care to preclude the possibility of drug-related funds reaching his bank account or being applied for his benefit. In the absence of inquiry he could have unwittingly received drug related funds ... To this extent at least he left himself, in my opinion, open to criticism for lack of prudence by a person holding the high office of Prime Minister.[8]

The main report exonerated Sir Lynden but it was the minority report, given by Bishop Gomez, that caused much controversy, and the Pindling family, much pain. The Pindlings were surprised and angry: Bishop Gomez had visited them and he had indicated that the Commission was going well and that everything was going to be all right. The minority report probably spurred many of the accusations about Sir Lynden. A *Miami Herald* reporter, Felicia R. Lee, wrote on 8 June 1987 that "some people say Pindling became greedy to satisfy Marguerite Pindling's lust for the high life of getting to London, New York and Miami for outrageous shopping sprees."[9]

At the time Lady Pindling said: "You just existed from day to day hoping that the nightmare would end. Living with this man, you know him. He's an only child whose parents taught him right from wrong – brought him up in the right way and like his father always said, keep your hands from picking and stealing and your tongue from evil speaking. Lynden Pindling, no. But that was the first step to undermine his Government."

Lady Pindling vigorously defended Sir Lynden's innocence. She was convinced that "it was a plot" to bring down him and his Government. Some of the witnesses giving evidence before the Commission were not believable. One accused Pindling of receiving a briefcase of money in a hotel at Paradise Island. Another accused him of accepting money in a brown paper bag at the airport. She said that that was "nonsense". He was determined to clear his name and hence the calling of the Commission. She said:

> Sir Lynden probably felt he was doing the right thing to clear his name not knowing that this man Ellicott came to bury him. It was like my husband was on trial and they already found him guilty. The trouble is, when we knew that drugs were passing through The Bahamas, he warned the Bahamian people. He appeared on

national television warning Bahamians that "if you get involved in drugs, you'll die." He told mothers not to come to him for their sons because he wouldn't be able to help them. He warned the people, then they came and accused him ... At that point when they discovered the drugs were coming through The Bahamas frequently, fast and furiously, it was probably too late. As you know, we are wide open. We are an island nation with miles and miles of water. If it was one land mass it might not have been so difficult. How are you going to protect all these islands?

The Pindlings found the accusations painful. Sir Lynden appeared strong and did not talk much about it. Dame Marguerite states that "the trust of the Bahamian people who believed in him and believed in his innocence helped him to come out of it." Everywhere he went there were newspapers with headlines "Paradise Lost – Nation for Sale". Of course the Opposition (FNM) jumped on that, hoping that "all the publicity and character assassination would help them to win the next election in 1987. I'm sure that took a toll on my husband."

Despite this, however, she says that "his conscience was clear. He was able to eat and sleep. He would even get his nap before going back to the Commission and when he came home at night that man slept like a baby."

The accusations against Pindling did have a negative impact on Pindling's Government. One way he reacted to the accusations was to pre-empt the imminent resignations of two Cabinet ministers, Hubert Ingraham and Perry Christie, by firing them – a power move by Pindling. He also accepted resignations of others including Arthur Hanna, Deputy Prime Minister and Minister of Finance, who was Pindling's closest political colleague. Hanna stated that he resigned "solely on a matter of principle".[10] Lady Pindling admitted that "really hurt" as Mr Hanna and Sir Lynden had a 40-year friendship, stretching back to schooldays in Nassau.

When asked if she thought that Sir Lynden ever thought of resigning, she stated "No, because it would make people believe that he was guilty of something and he was determined to prove his innocence ... he was not going to let them get away with it but this family – we suffered in the meantime – the pain, the humiliation." He also received support from the PLPs in the Family Islands.

I'll never forget the women from the Family Islands, they would call. I remember ... one morning, Mary Dames from George Town called to say "I just called to say I love you" ... it was a popular song then and it gave him strength. He was encouraged by the support he received from around The Bahamas. Ann Grant of West End, Grand Bahama often called. The Baptist women came and prayed and laid hands on him. The poor man, I thought they were going to injure him. They just wanted him to go out in faith knowing that the truth would come out ...

The women of Bethel Baptist Church, especially Dr Doris Johnson's colleagues, Mother Rand, Harriet McDonald and Beryl Francis Culmer, were most supportive. They represented the Willing Workers' Band. Often they would be waiting for him when he returned home after work to offer prayers and to anoint him with olive oil, covering his head, hands and feet. These gestures gave him strength. Mother Davis of the Dixie Church of God on Wulff Road also helped to sustain the Pindlings during this difficult period.

William Thompson, priest in charge of St Agnes Anglican where Lady Pindling was (and still is) a member and worshipped, was also very supportive. Lady Pindling said that "Father Willie was in a class by himself. He used to come and sit with Sir Lynden. I could only hear talking and laughing in there."

It was a trying time, with accusations against Sir Lynden swirling all over the world, the new house owned by the Pindlings constantly being photographed and American helicopters frequently flying at low altitudes over their home. She admits that they were "deeply hurt especially by the fact that some of their 'own people' [PLP supporters] believed he was guilty. Sir Lynden never talked about his feelings, but for me as a wife and mother, the pain was deep ... but thank God for the churches and the women especially. They helped us to survive."

She adds: "We had to go through all of that but still they haven't found anything ... I don't remember any concrete evidence coming out saying yes, he knew and he admitted to knowing ... nothing like that happened but by the grace of God he survived. In fact, I remember Eagleburger, the American Secretary of State, saying that he never had any proof of any wrongdoing by Sir Lynden."

In 1989 Sir Lynden, in an effort to "transform" his and The Bahamas' image regarding drug-trafficking in the archipelago, gave a stunning speech to members of the 1989 Commonwealth Heads of Government Meeting (CHOGM) held in Kuala Lumpur, Malaysia. Informing his colleagues of the positive efforts made by The Bahamas in curbing the trade, some on its own and others bilaterally with the United States and other Caribbean countries, he proposed a plan. Supported by Jamaica and other Caribbean countries, his plan included the international community – "a multilateral campaign" aimed at hindering the cultivation, transportation and profitability of the nefarious trade.

On the positive side, the Royal Bahamas Police Force and the Royal Bahamas Defence Force were expanded and made more professional through the creation of a police college, the establishment of a special drug training course and the expansion of the Defence Force's fleet. Relations and cooperation with the United States agencies improved. In 1990 Paul Adderley, Minister of National Security, claimed that cocaine traffic had greatly diminished. By the mid-1990s, relations between the United States and The Bahamas had improved even more and the DEA, FBI and US Coast Guard worked closely with the Bahamas police and defence forces, sharing information and a surveillance system that included "sophisticated radars hovering in captive balloons over Grand Bahama, Exuma and Inagua".[11]

Dame Marguerite comments: "It is in the people's minds to this day. Persons who knew the man knew that Pindling was not that kind of person. He would not cover up. Cover up a wrong for what? Anyway, time is a great healer." But "even after all these years, it pains me to this day to have to read all of the unkind reports from the foreign press accusing my husband of not being a drug lord but harbouring druggies in this country."

8
Memorable Moments in the International Arena

The Coronation of Elizabeth II in 1953 symbolized the transition from the "old Empire of dependent colonies and the limited all-white associations of Dominions joined in the 1930s" to the beginning of "a new multi-ethnic Commonwealth of independent nations voluntarily bonded together, most of them willingly acknowledging the sovereignty of the Queen".[1]

A meeting of Commonwealth prime ministers "accompanied" the Coronation, and non-white leaders of former colonies and dependent territories, including Jawaharlal Nehru of India, attended. Lynden Pindling, who had just completed law studies and had asked his parents for permission to stay for the Coronation, was among the millions who were in London for the grand event and Michael Craton stated that it left a "lasting imprint" on him. Pindling, of course, would lead The Bahamas into Majority Rule and Independence and become its first Prime Minister and architect of the modern Commonwealth of The Bahamas. By that time, Lynden Pindling had at his side a beautiful and intelligent wife, Marguerite (née McKenzie) who would bring glamour and, after a brief time, political savvy.

As the wife of the Prime Minister, Mrs Pindling travelled a lot. She usually accompanied her husband to Commonwealth Heads of Government Meetings which were held biennially. As noted in Chapter 5, she and her husband attended the first meeting of the Commonwealth Heads of Government held in Ottawa. There they met Sir Lynden's old friend Pierre Trudeau, then Prime Minister of Canada. Dame Marguerite recalls the opening of the Conference in Ottawa:

> *I found it very exciting, the morning of the meeting which was a brand new experience ... As we sat I looked around the room and saw all the flags of the other countries and said to my husband "Gee, we are up front." He said "Don't be silly, it's arranged alphabetically, that's why you're there." It was Australia, The Bahamas and Canada ... It was a very proud moment for The Bahamas. This was its first CHOGM. It was a tremendous privilege, sitting there with world leaders, some of whom I'd never heard of but I got to know them after a while.*

She also remembers the dinner and meeting Her Majesty Queen Elizabeth II:

> *I think there was a dinner that evening – it's all like a dream now and Her Majesty was receiving her guests and so when it came to my turn – I guess I was all excited after Independence ... Prince Charles had just left and so I thought I could just walk up to Her Majesty and just talk ... She asked me about Independence and we were talking, talking ... I told her how well it went and how excited the people were and that our first Governor-General had just been sworn in. It was all about Independence.*
>
> *I was very exhilarated and I told her that everything went smoothly and Prince Charles was warmly received by the Bahamian people and we were all very proud that he was able to come to celebrate with us – the birth of our new nation – a new Bahamas ... I also told her that I thought he enjoyed himself and she asked "Did he behave?" I said, "He certainly did."*
>
> *I felt she had already heard much of what I was telling her. Obviously it was time for someone else ... she just looked up at her lady-in-waiting and then I realized it was time to go. I thought, "Oh my God, what have I done, perhaps I have talked too much."*

During the Conference in Canada she met Mrs Julius Nyerere of Tanzania, a very quiet lady, for the first time. Her husband was the most senior Commonwealth leader. Dame Marguerite recalls: "I found that during all of the Heads of Government Meetings and the official dinners with Her Majesty, she spent a lot of time with the African women ... Mrs Nyerere and Mrs Kaunda of Zambia were the senior wives ... and the Queen spent more time talking to them than the younger wives ... of course I also met Mrs Margaret Trudeau, wife of the Prime Minister of Canada."

The Pindlings spent a week in Ottawa, and then went to the traditional CHOGM Retreat after which their children joined them. She reminisces: "It was a very pleasant experience ... an education and a learning experience for me ... I learnt the dos and don'ts of CHOGM. Because we were the newest Nation ... we were the centre of attraction."

Marguerite Pindling attended her second CHOGM, held in Jamaica, in 1975. Michael Manley was then Prime Minister. He had just remarried. He and his wife had honeymooned in The Bahamas, at a location recommended by Mr Pindling. Mrs Pindling found it strange that when she was introduced to Mrs Beverley Manley she did not comment on her stay in

The Bahamas. In fact she was "rather cold". Dame Marguerite's memories of the Jamaica meeting are not happy ones. She recalls:

> *They arranged a seminar for wives of prime ministers somewhere in the country and it took almost an hour to get there ... When we got there, I could remember the wife of the Australian Prime Minister (Guy Whitlam) ... she was the chairperson and I was out of my depth. It was my first time in Jamaica and it was hot and I perspired a lot and my dress got stained. Following the seminar was a luncheon at Jamaica House of which we had not been informed. I realized that I could not attend in what I was wearing ... I was soaking wet and by the time I arrived at Jamaica House, the luncheon was over. I never remembered being given a programme or an invitation.*

She also admits that the subjects discussed were very academic and she felt like people "put her down":

> *An incident took place – I can't remember which of the ladies said it to me – it was during a function, she said "You Bahamians have no identity or culture, you're too Americanized. You are a people of service." At that point I vigorously defended Bahamians. I was arguing that we were not Americanized ... I think that now we're too Americanized. I turned to defend my country and my people and so I was left feeling distraught and alone. What an experience for me.*

Fortunately, Mrs Senorita Strachan, mother of talented playwright, poet, novelist and film maker and college professor Ian Strachan, was studying at the University of the West Indies (accompanied by all her children). The Pindlings visited the Bahamian students at UWI and Mrs Pindling related the story to her. Mrs Strachan said, "Oh, don't pay any attention to these people, they think they know everything and they know better than everybody in the world." Senorita Strachan's words comforted Mrs Pindling and she felt somewhat relieved. Being new, she did not know the people. Lynden Pindling, on the other hand, whose father was Jamaican, knew a number of Jamaicans including some who were politicians, such as Dudley Thompson, Hugh Shearer and P. J. Patterson. He was also acquainted with George Barbar, deputy chair of the Jamaica Labour Party, a protégé of Bustamente, Leader of the Jamaica Labour Party, who was a close friend from the 1960s until Pindling's death.

In 1977 the Commonwealth Heads of Government Meeting (CHOGM) was held in London. It was a special occasion as the Queen was celebrating her Silver Jubilee. Dame Marguerite remembers that they dined at Buckingham Palace. She recalls that she had one drink and "not too much to eat because of the excitement".

Lady Pindling did not attend the next two CHOGMs which were held in Australia (1981) and India in 1983. In fact Sir Lynden did not attend the CHOGM in Australia because of the "pressure of work".[2] However, he attended the CHOGM in India. It was there that Sir Lynden made a successful bid for The Bahamas to host CHOGM in 1985. It came at a peculiar time – right after the Commission of Inquiry sessions. Lady Pindling realized the hosting of CHOGM "vindicated Sir Lynden, in a way because it was quite a success, although we still faced the Opposition".

Indeed the Opposition Free National Movement kept up a constant attack against Sir Lynden Pindling and the PLP. The House of Assembly did not meet between June and November 1985 and this gave the Government time to plan for CHOGM which was held in Nassau during October of that year. The meetings were well organized, as were security measures and media coverage. CHOGM, which was held in the Cable Beach Hotel, was a success both professionally and socially. Moreover, the outcome of the discussions which resulted in the Nassau Declaration of Principles, in Michael Craton's words, "enhanced the prestige" of the Bahamian Government and Sir Lynden Pindling, the Prime Minister. The presence of Her Majesty Queen Elizabeth II was an added advantage and The Bahamas attracted international attention.

While the Government basked in the spotlight, the Opposition attracted attention by its boycott of the business sessions and social events. The FNM continued its demonstrations using placards with critical messages including "L.O. MUST GO" and "The Chief is a Thief". However, Bahamians generally were "excited" and impressed by the presence of The Queen and Sir Lynden's "imperturbable geniality" and "the elegant charm of his wife".[3]

The Opposition were vigorously picketing on Marlborough Street which was en route to Prince George Dock where the *Britannia* was docked. For security reasons several of the leaders, including Prime Minister Ghandi of India, President Kaunda of Zambia and the President of the Maldives and several others were taken by boat to attend the state dinner on the royal yacht. Unfortunately, it was very rough (some were sick) and they were an hour late.

> The Queen was on the Britannia waiting – as I stepped on the deck of the Britannia she stood like Queen Victoria and said: "Where were you?" I was very embarrassed and ashamed. The Queen, not surprisingly, was up to date as to what was going on in The Bahamas. She said: "I did see the placards with the 'Chief is a Thief.'"

Lady Pindling hosted a very elegant women's luncheon on 17 October 1985 in the Crown Ballroom, Paradise Island. During the luncheon, which was attended by local dignitaries, including Lady Symonette, and wives of delegates, Lady Pindling welcomed all who attended, especially her guests from sister Commonwealth countries. She noted the challenges, referring to "millions of ... South African women" who "are shackled and shattered by the pangs of modern day slavery". She continued:

> *While there are only two women sitting around the table with other Commonwealth Heads, the collective voices of women must ring out more loudly than ever before. As historic victims of sexism and gender-based discrimination, we must all utilize every opportunity to denounce racism and colour-based discrimination. If Commonwealth women do not do it, who will? I am hopeful that events such as this will serve to strengthen the ties between us and amplify the common thread that unifies us. I have no doubt that when this meeting has ended, we will all have been enriched by the CHOGM experience in The Bahamas.*

Each wife of the Heads of Government received an Ivy Simms straw bag which Lady Pindling personally ordered. The bags were lined with different designs of Androsia (a Bahamian batik fabric). There was also a length of Androsia in each bag. The male staff of the *Britannia* each received a blue Androsia shirt. When Lady Pindling met Mr Fellows, the Queen's Secretary, in London, he said that his son had taken his shirt and he asked for a replacement. Among the gifts which were given to the Heads of Government were china plates with The Bahamas Coat of Arms and crystal paper weights with the Coat of Arms at the bottom.

Lady Pindling also hosted another elegant luncheon on a yacht, *The Lady Alice*, owned by George and Alice Barbar. It was docked at Lyford Cay where the traditional CHOGM retreat was held. The Pindlings lived at Lyford Cay for the retreat that weekend.

A highlight for Lady Pindling was the Queen's visit to Fresh Creek, Andros. She remembers the voyage back on the *Britannia* when just six of them, including the Queen, had a cosy lunch.

Although she was involved mainly in social events, Lady Pindling was aware that the critical situation of apartheid in South Africa was one of the most important issues discussed at the Nassau CHOGM. As Michael Craton notes, Lynden Pindling skilfully negotiated with some of the senior Commonwealth members including Australia, New Zealand and Canada, persuading Heads to vote in favour of sanctions against South Africa. His efforts were rewarded as the Nassau CHOGM 1985 produced "the declaration against *Apartheid* and the endorsement of sanctions".[4] As Craton states: "Nelson Mandela himself was gratefully to mark this as an important breakthrough on the way to effective international sanctions, which in turn led to his own release from prison, the dismantling of apartheid, the realization of black majority rule, and his election as President of South Africa in 1992."[5]

Lynden Pindling's contribution to the CHOGM 1985 and the Nassau Declaration won him an invitation to membership of the Eminent Persons Group which visited South Africa in 1986 and submitted a report of its findings. Pindling and The Bahamas were therefore indelibly associated with the events that led to the release of Nelson Mandela, the dismantling of apartheid, black majority rule and South Africa's admission to the Commonwealth.[6]

It was after the PLP and Sir Lynden lost power that Nelson Mandela visited Nassau. Dame Marguerite remembers that his aide called on them to ask for an invitation to dinner. With the help of friends such as Vernice Cooper and her own family, she was able hurriedly to organize a dinner. In addition, the Pindlings hosted a reception following the dinner to which a larger number of friends and colleagues were invited. She and Sir Lynden were also invited to a dinner in honour of Mandela hosted by Prime Minister Hubert Ingraham.

The CHOGM in Zimbabwe was the last one attended by the Pindlings. The country was then (in 1991) flourishing under President Mugabe, being known as the breadbasket of Africa. Lady Pindling noticed that the capital, Harare, was well laid out. She remembers the jacaranda trees which lined the main streets in the city. They gave the area a smoke-like atmosphere. More vivid was her memory of the accident in which she and Sir Lynden were involved. A group of delegates was returning from the CHOGM retreat which had been held near to the Victoria Falls. She and Sir Lynden were seated in the front of the bus on which they were travelling. As they came to an intersection, a jeep sped across their path. The driver slammed the brakes and they were thrown forward. Lady Pindling fell on the floor on her stomach and received a cut on her shin bone. Sir Lynden fared better and was not injured. However, an ambulance took them all to the hospital where they were put in wheelchairs, x-rayed and given medicine where necessary. All involved were very fortunate.

In late 1982 Lynden Pindling was nominated for a knighthood. At the age of 52, Pindling was the "father" of the House of Assembly and the "longest-serving head of government in the Commonwealth Caribbean".[7] The honour was a display of approval from the entire Bahamian Cabinet which in fact initiated British honours in The Bahamas although they are bestowed by the sovereign, in this case, Queen Elizabeth II. His predecessor, Sir Roland Symonette, the first Premier of The Bahamas, also received a knighthood but before he became Premier.

The honour, a KCMG or Knight Commander of the Order of St Michael and St George, was bestowed on Pindling in the New Year's 1983 list. It was announced on New Year's Eve in 1982. Lady Pindling, when asked about her reactions, stated that "I was happy for him. I thought he was deserving of it. I guess in the excitement I just cried. Like he said, 'he did it for me' which I didn't understand but later I realized what he meant." She emphasized that Sir Lynden did not want recognition – that was not what he was working for. He believed his cause was right and he was determined to help his people. He probably knew "he would be recognized one day" but he never sought recognition.

However, the Pindlings "made the most of it". A jet was put at their disposal and a group of PLP supporters and friends travelled to London, including Rubie and Kendal Nottage, Vernice Cooper, Beverley Whitfield, Sir Lynden's parents and other Pindling family members including Alice McKenzie, Lady Pindling's sister-in-law. Alice played a major role in Lady Pindling's life. She was a good travelling companion and helped her tremendously.

The actual ceremony at Buckingham Palace was very moving. Unfortunately only Lady Pindling and Lynden's parents, Arnold and Viola Pindling, were allowed into Buckingham Palace to witness the ceremony. Lady Pindling was particularly happy that Sir Lynden was able to take his parents to Buckingham Palace. She recalls the experience:

> On arrival they told us to take our coats to the cloakroom. We did not know where the cloakroom was at Buckingham Palace so we sauntered along the passageway. Sir Lynden's Mom and I had to go upstairs, she's looking at me and I'm looking at her. We finally found someone to show us ... we sat in the balcony. I can remember she [The Queen] said something to him [Sir Lynden] but I don't remember what it was. Then she tapped him on his shoulders and said, "Rise, Sir Lynden." I looked at his father and he was beaming. His mother never said very much but I am sure she was quite pleased as well. But grandfather could not contain his excitement. Two men, stalwarts in the PLP from North Andros, also received Queen's honours that day.

Nancy Oakes held a luncheon at Claridge's after the ceremony and in the evening, their friend Edward St George of the Grand Bahama Port Authority hosted a dinner for the Pindlings at fashionable Annabelle's, inviting a host of Bahamians. Dame Marguerite recalls: "Everyone was crying." Monique, their youngest child, spoke and also Trevor Whylly and Charlie Major Jr. "I was crying – tears of happiness and Sir Lynden just sat there with a dead pan face and shrugged his shoulders – 'the little boy from East Street'."

Two years before receiving the knighthood, the Pindlings attended the Royal Wedding of His Royal Highness Prince Charles and Lady Diana Spencer on 21 July 1981. Sir Gerald, then Governor-General of The Bahamas, and Lady Cash also were invited and along with the Pindlings represented The Bahamas. In addition, Mr and Mrs Henry Sands of Savannah Sound, Eleuthera, who had baked bread for Prince Charles while he vacationed at Windermere in Eleuthera, attended.

On that visit to London, the Pindlings stayed at the Hyde Park Hotel and the night before the wedding had dinner at Buckingham Palace. Lady Pindling's dinner companions were Cabinet Minister Michael Heseltine and the Duchess of Kent. Lady Pindling remarked that she always ate before going to Buckingham Palace for dinner, as the servings were conservative and you did not get a second helping!

At the dinner table, Mr Heseltine thought she was propositioning him. "We were talking and I innocently remarked 'Gee, you should see my ankle' or something like that, and he said 'Are you propositioning me?' So I replied 'Heaven forbid, no!' and everyone laughed. It was so funny."

Lady Pindling was accompanied by Vernice Cooper, who helped to dress her. Her hairdresser Michelangelo Bacelli was also in London at the time. She was stunning as usual and found the wedding, held at St Paul's Cathedral, magical – like a fairy tale. Princess Diana was "just so beautiful – absolutely radiant".

The Pindlings had excellent seats along with the other Commonwealth prime ministers, governors-general and presidents. Dame Marguerite says that they had a marvellous view of the bride and groom. She remarks sadly: "It's a pity it ended the way it did. The wedding was really spectacular." They stayed in London for a few days following the wedding and during that time, dined with Lord and Lady Pritchard at the Dorchester Hotel. It was a most exciting and enjoyable trip – she felt privileged to have been afforded the opportunity given to her by the Bahamian people.

9
Two Defeats and Retirement from Politics

The Progressive Liberal Party suffered a devastating defeat to the Free National Movement in the general election of 19 August 1992. Winning 63,181 votes or 55.7 per cent of the total, to the PLP's 42,043 or 46.6 per cent, the FNM captured 31 seats to the PLP's 18.

Sir Lynden won his seat in Kemp's Bay, South Andros, decisively, as did Hubert Ingraham in Cooper's Town, Abaco. Ingraham, Leader of the FNM, had served in the Pindling Cabinet between 1982 and 1985 before being fired during the drug crisis for criticizing the leadership over the issue. Sir Lynden, who had led his party to victory in the last six elections (1967, 1968, 1972, 1977, 1982 and 1987), although disappointed with the results, graciously conceded the defeat with the words: "The people of this great little democracy have spoken in a most dignified and elegant manner and the voice of the people is the voice of God."[1]

Lady Pindling also felt disappointed and hurt. She admits: "I never knew what it was to lose an election [except for 1962] ... For 25 years we were on the world stage and so we lost ... This could be attributed to several factors including the Gulf War. People were grumbling. The defeat was humbling ... Hubert Ingraham came along with the things they wanted to hear but you know, the time had come for the PLP."

She states that she felt a bit uneasy just before the 1992 election. Sir Lynden did not say anything but she "got a feeling". She continues:

> *But the funniest thing happened on election morning. Our aide was late getting here because we had to go and vote and get down to Kemp's Bay, so when he came I said, "Well Mr Kemp, why are you late, you know we have to get off to Kemp's Bay this morning, is this a good or bad omen, does this mean we are going to lose the election? He said nothing and just looked at me. Those were my words but I had the strangest feeling all day in Kemp's Bay ... My left eye kept jumping all day long and I saw the change in people. It wasn't that outgoing feeling; the excitement wasn't quite right. I am sure my husband felt that too but of course you know he didn't say.*

Asked why she thought the FNM won, she attributes the victory to Hubert Ingraham's "invigorating campaign and his ability to sway some of our supporters who had become disillusioned". She also thinks that the candidates on the PLP side had become complacent and that Sir Lynden did not campaign for them the way he normally did. Sir Lynden admitted that the PLP candidates did not work hard enough. Dame Marguerite also believes that it was "divine intervention; I think the Lord was telling us something and it was time to take a break and let someone else govern ... so that the people could see the difference. This fellow [Hubert Ingraham] came in with a more exciting point of view and raised the hopes of the people, especially the young people who had no loyalties to the PLP, that they could do more for them ... The tide had turned."

The Pindlings were in South Andros when the results were announced. They felt terrible. To add to their shock, Sir Lynden's opponent, FNM candidate Ronald Bosfield, was arrogant and nasty. "He came down on a truck with some young fellows with their torches lit and drove right up to our cottage and into the yard with the torches and stood under the window that night tauntingly, shouting 'Go home Pindling, leave Andros'."

Feeling extremely disappointed and let down, the Pindlings stayed in Kemp's Bay for two days before returning to Nassau. Their elder daughter Michelle, who had contested the Yamacraw seat in opposition to Janet Bostwick, lost. It was difficult for everyone. The Broadcasting Corporation (ZNS) was awaiting their arrival and Sir Lynden had to make a statement.

Party officers and supporters were at the airport. But what could he say to them? Dame Marguerite states: "That's when he decided it was time for him to move on. He was resigning as Leader because he said he couldn't see himself carrying on any further. Some of the candidates blamed him for the loss."

However, four months later at the Party's Annual Convention in January 1993, Sir Lynden agreed to stay on as Leader. This decision came after members and supporters of the party "begged and pleaded" with him "asking him not to go ... everybody was breaking down ... Members of the party wept, asking him to reconsider his decision. About a week or so later, he told them he would think about it because he had to see if that was what he really wanted to do again." Dame Marguerite recounts what Sir Lynden said at the time: "I think I've had enough and since I'm to blame, I'll get out of the way and let them carry on by themselves."

This all happened at a meeting in the grounds of Workers' House. On this particular night it was pouring with rain. Members did not want him to leave them. It was heart-wrenching to watch as members and supporters mobbed him. They were crying and so was Sir Lynden.

Dame Marguerite says that Sir Lynden was determined that he would resign as Leader but stalwarts and supporters of the PLP begged him to stay. At first, he said that he would remain only until they found themselves another Leader. That is when Bernard Nottage, a former Cabinet Minister, aspired to the leadership. Sir Lynden's supporters intervened, Bernard Nottage pulled back. Sir Lynden Pindling decided to stay on as Leader, giving a most eloquent speech at the Thirty-seventh Annual PLP Convention held in January 1993. According to Dame Marguerite, though, "Sir Lynden did it half-heartedly; he really didn't want to stay on. He was ready to move on."

Life in Opposition changed dramatically for the Pindlings. Dame Marguerite explains:

> Our lives ... changed; it came to an abrupt end: we were as though in a daze. I didn't know anything about defeat since 1967. Suddenly you realize you have no driver, you have to do things for yourself. Aides had done so much for us, planning and making our arrangements. These were taken away from us. Many times we would go out and come back and couldn't get in the house because we did not have a key. Suddenly you realize you have to wake up – this is reality!

She states that people from the top down were unkind to them. In the heat of the moment Prime Minister Ingraham alluded to the Pindlings' position: "the dog gone, the maid gone ...". Lady Pindling felt that this was an insult to Sir Lynden who had made such a contribution to the development of The Bahamas. She states: "Rather than the way he behaved, the new Prime Minister coming on stream should have been more gracious and thanked the previous holder of the office for what he had done for the country; he should have ask for his support to build on what had already been achieved."

She was sadly disappointed by Mr Ingraham's arrogance, unkindness, lack of respect and behaviour towards Sir Lynden at that time (it would change later) and she blamed him for influencing the population generally – "they were so rude". Similarly, she was appalled at the behaviour of the ordinary citizens. Some people came to the gate of the Pindlings' house and shouted "get out of our house", not realizing that the family owned their home.

They also were criticized for living in luxurious suites at a hotel in Freeport when they visited Grand Bahama. Led by Deborah Bartlett, a ZNS reporter, television crews took viewers through the hotel suites, which seemed quite ordinary – quite modest. There was nothing to criticize!

People passed the Pindlings' house on trucks and shouted obscenities. Dame Marguerite remarks:

> It was "an awakening" for me ... and suddenly I realized, my God, do they hate him that much? I would stand in the yard dumbfounded. A humbling experience and my heart bled for my husband – I don't remember him commenting at the time but he's human and I know he felt it ... He had once said not to expect any gratitude because there would be none. We suffered at the hands of the people who had once supported us – they were vicious.

Even the attitude of the policemen on duty changed. Dame Marguerite recalls: "When we came back from Andros after we had lost, the officers on duty here at the house became very slack and disrespectful. They would sit down at the gate and play dominoes. I went in the back [yard] for some reason and they were washing their cars and saw me standing there and never said 'good morning'."

An incident which was most humiliating took place on Bahamasair during Sir Lynden's illness. Lady Pindling had accompanied Sir Lynden to Miami to undergo medical tests. He had been hospitalized at Baptist Hospital for a night and had just been released. Mr Dashville Williams, who was to drive them to the airport, was late getting back to the hotel because of heavy traffic. Hence they were late arriving at the airport. Dame Marguerite recalls:

> We were late but they held the plane. As we boarded the aircraft a few passengers shouted: "That's what you held up this plane for? He needs to be on time like everybody else, he's not the Prime Minister now!" It was so embarrassing and they carried on for about half an hour. Sir Lynden was ill and was in much pain ... The stewardess spoke to the passengers, asking them to be quiet and they refused so she said: "I'm going to speak to the pilot", who in turn threatened to return to the gate and have the troublemakers removed.

Sir Lynden sat quietly on the plane, not saying a word. She says that her "heart melted for him. I felt like an ant but I had to put on a brave face."

The day after the Pindlings returned from Andros after the defeat, the official car was sent to the police barracks and in Dame Marguerite's words they were "left defenceless – ordinary Bahamians again". One of Sir Lynden's aides, Inspector Rolle, stayed on until September and was then recalled, and the Pindlings found themselves alone, just "the two of us". Neither had driven in many years and did not have their own transport (except for the Rolls Royce which they only used for special occasions) for some time until some friends bought them a used car. But there was no driver. The family, including Dame Marguerite's siblings, Priscilla Williams, Doris Albury, Julie Ambrister and Sidney McKenzie, was supportive and came to their rescue. The children and Lady Pindling's sister-in-law, Alice McKenzie, would alternate in taking Sir Lynden to and from the office and transporting him for lunch and back to the office. It is not well known, but Dr Frank Walkine lent Sir Lynden a car (a Jaguar) for a number of weeks after his defeat.

Socially, life changed for Lady Pindling. She did not attend many public events. She says:

> *We were never invited. If you were, you received the invitation the very day or the day after. When you did accept an invitation, you got the feeling – the atmosphere was so thick ... You did not feel welcomed ... They turned their backs to you when they saw you coming and you know me, I am very bold politically because you know I have no fear of them and I would walk up to them and say, "How are you today?" – embarrass them.*

She felt that since the Opposition was in power, it should not be afraid of her. She admits: "But it happened and we were slighted and we never accepted too many of the engagements because I think the Government invited us half-heartedly, hoping that we wouldn't show."

When Sir Lynden retired in 1997, a dinner was held in his honour, hosted by Sir Orville Turnquest, then Governor-General and Lady Turnquest. That was the "first and last time we were invited for dinner" at Government House while the PLP was in Opposition between 1992 and 2002.

Between 1992 and 1997, Sir Lynden served as Leader of the Opposition. Perry Christie and Bernard Nottage were elected co-Deputy Leaders of the PLP, posts they held until Sir Lynden's retirement in 1997. At that time, an election for the leadership was held and after a bitter battle Perry Christie, supported by Pindling, emerged as the winner. Many supporters were very critical of Sir Lynden for his preference.

Sir Lynden as Leader faced "the brunt of the new Government's campaign of recrimination".[2] Top of their agenda was a Commission of Inquiry into the "inefficiency, mismanagement and corruption in government-run corporations" including Bahamasair, BATELCO, BEC and the Hotel Corporation – which had been chaired by Prime Minister Lynden Pindling for 15 years. Sir Lynden was examined in May 1994 by the Commission regarding, especially, the work of the Hotel Corporation. While admitting that he had accepted financial assistance from friends and well-wishers, he emphasized that he had not accepted any bribes or kickbacks nor received money under the table. In the end, "no charges were laid, let alone proved" against Sir Lynden, and the Commission of Inquiry "petered out".[3]

Lady Pindling, mortified that her husband was again put under such scrutiny, was convinced that the pressure he endured helped to worsen his cancer. "I truly believe that the cancer had started and that the Commission of Inquiry helped to accelerate it because he complained then about a pain in his shoulder."

In 1996, Sir Lynden, who had a record of excellent health, became ill and was diagnosed with prostate cancer in the early stages. Lady Pindling naturally was very upset, but ever supportive during his treatment and throughout his entire illness. The children also rallied round to assist in any way possible.

Despite his illness, Sir Lynden led the PLP into the 14 March 1997 general election. It was a landslide for the FNM, which won 34 of the parliamentary seats to the PLP's 6. Sir Lynden, who was re-elected for South Andros for the eighth time, was the only PLP to win a seat in a Family Island constituency. After experiencing such a stinging defeat Sir Lynden agreed to step down as Party Leader and Member of Parliament. On Monday 7 July 1997 he resigned his seat after delivering an eloquent, moving and powerful speech. Paying tribute to parliamentarians who had died, he thanked God first and his family for their "unflinching love and loyalty". Sir Lynden also apologized to his family for not being able to protect them completely from "poisoned slings and arrows" of the "outer world" to which he belonged.

Sir Lynden had special words for his wife of 41 years:

> As for my wife, Madam Speaker, a very special word, if I may. It has been my singular good fortune to have at my side since the time of my entry into electoral politics in 1956 to my exit in 1997, a princess whose bearing, grace and charm made her the toast of four continents and a lady whose fortitude in the face of the most daunting adversities, and whose unwavering devotion to me and what I stood for, contributed mightily to my survival and my success in public life. To Marguerite, my wife, my lover, my homemaker, and my best friend of forty-one years, let me say this then, that for her support, her understanding, her tender and constant care and her boundless love and devotion, I am grateful beyond measure."[4]

10
Life after Sir Lynden

Dame Marguerite recalls that the family became aware of Sir Lynden's illness in about February 1996, when he complained of pain in his right shoulder. In March of that year after attending Carnival with his elder son, Obi, he visited Dr Walkine, who referred him to a doctor in Miami. At first nothing was found, but the pain persisted. Eventually he was referred to an oncologist at Baptist Hospital in Miami, Florida, where he took a series of tests. The doctors thought the mass in his stomach was cancerous. However, on the advice of Perry Christie, Sir Lynden was seen by Dr Dwayne Sands, who admitted him to Doctor's Hospital in Nassau and tested the mass in his stomach, samples of which were sent to John Hopkins Hospital in Baltimore where Dr Sands had trained. Much to Lady Pindling's relief, Dr Sands called to say that the mass was benign. However, on checking with kidney specialist Dr Robin Roberts, it was discovered that Sir Lynden's PSA was high. He was admitted to Doctors Hospital in Nassau, where tests confirmed that he had prostate cancer which had spread to the bones. Shortly afterwards he was admitted for treatment at Johns Hopkins Hospital.

Lady Pindling related how kind people were, especially Dashville (Dashie) Williams, a close friend and businessman who lived in Freeport. She had nothing but praise for Dashie:

> *I want to give Dashie the credit for staying with Sir Lynden. Dashie travelled everywhere with him, when everybody else forsook him ... he accompanied him on every trip he made out of the country – paying his own way until '97 when it was agreed by the Cabinet to give him a stipend to assist him. That is after Sir Lynden had retired and Dashie travelled with Pindling until the day he was not able to move.*

When others heard that Sir Lynden had to undergo ten weeks of radiation treatment, personal friends such as Patricia Mortimer, Annie Ralston, Frankie and Sharon Wilson and Richard Demeritte gave generously. Calsey Johnson visited, and Richard Demeritte arranged for Sir Lynden's transport for the ten weeks he was in Baltimore. Leslie Miller painted their house, changing the colour from pink to white. Obie Wilchcombe, Felix Bowe, Charles Major Jr. and Skeeter Collins also assisted.

Lady Pindling was appreciative of the friends who "came to his rescue financially" but said there was one "outstanding contribution" that would stay with her forever:

> *We had a rally the night before [they left for Baltimore for Sir Lynden to receive radiation treatment] and in the crowd I felt someone hitting me on my leg. In the crowd you don't know who's doing it and I kept looking around. There was a lady standing right in front of me and she had a knot in her forehead and she kept hitting me and she put $40 in my hand to help with Sir Lynden's medical bills. I don't know to this day who she was. A very simple, ordinary woman who wanted to make her contribution and I would be forever grateful to her. I hope one day, if she reads the book she will come forward and identify herself because I was very grateful for that.*

On Sir Lynden's return to Nassau, a motorcade was arranged by the PLP to welcome him home.

Sir Lynden's health worsened after the 1997 election. He visited doctors at Johns Hopkins again, the last visit being in July 2000. Lady Pindling sensed then that his doctor was saying goodbye when he spoke to Sir Lynden, saying "Old friend, what can I do for you today?" Michelle Pindling-Sands said that she saw it in his face and tone of voice and knew he was saying goodbye. Dame Marguerite says: "I am sure Sir Lynden realized. Only me – I was just out of it. After he came home, he started going downhill."

Soon after returning home, Sir Lynden called his wife and children together and told them "I am going to die." He gave instructions to them about his business matters, the house and property, and urged the children to keep close to one another and to take care of their mother. Dame Marguerite admits that she did not want to hear this, and so blocked it out. She regrets that she did not listen. Leslie related to her what he had told them.

The meeting occurred about a month before his death. Lady Pindling knew what was happening but found it hard to face up to it. She kept herself very busy and assisted him all she could. A week before his death, Garet Finlayson and Bradley Roberts spent about two hours talking with him. However, by this time he was weakening and tired easily.

On the Wednesday before he died she noticed him looking out at the garden. On Thursday he talked to Sean McWeeney downstairs and arranged to give power of attorney to his children. On Friday he was confined to bed, but had visitors. Prime Minister the Rt Honourable Hubert Ingraham and Norman Solomon, businessman and former member of the House of Assembly, visited early in the day. Opposition Leader the Hon. Perry

122. Governor-General Sir Gerald Cash, Lady Cash, HRH Prince Charles, Princess Diana, Lady Pindling and Sir Lynden at Government House, Nassau, 1982

123. Lady Pindling and Sir Lynden at CHOGM, Nassau, 1985

124. Lady Pindling, Sir Gerald Cash, HM Queen Elizabeth II, Sir Lynden and Lady Cash on the Royal Yacht *Britannia*; CHOGM, Nassau, 1985

125. Mrs Arnold Smith, wife of the secretary to CHOGM, Mrs Julius Nyerere and Mrs Lynden Pindling in October 1973

126. The Pindlings, Prime Minister Hubert Ingraham, Lady Darling and Sir Clifford Darling and Nelson Mandela at Government House, March 1993. *Photo: Franklyn G. Ferguson*

127. Nelson Mandela visits the Pindlings, 1993

128. Mr Lynden and Mrs Marguerite Pindling before attending a dinner at Buckingham Palace, just before the wedding of Prince Charles and Lady Diana Spencer on 29 July 1981

129. The Pindlings (top left) at the Royal Wedding, 1981

130. Lady Pindling and Prime Minister Margaret Thatcher at CHOGM, Nassau, 1985

131. Sir Lynden, Mrs Viola Pindling (his mother), Lady Pindling and Arnold Pindling (his father) after Sir Lynden received his knighthood in June 1983

132. Lady Pindling with the wives of Heads of Government in Harare, Zimbabwe, in 1991; Lady Pindling is sixth from the right on the second row

133. Lady Pindling being presented to HM the Queen at CHOGM, 1985; Sir Lynden and Sir Clifford Darling look on

134. Sir Lynden and Lady Pindling entertain Mrs Rosa Parks at their home, Lynmar, Prospect Ridge, New Providence

135. Mrs Marguerite Pindling and others attend a service conducted by Rev. Dr. Billy Graham at the Queen Elizabeth Sports Centre, New Providence

136. Rev. Billy Graham speaking at the Templeton Prize Ceremony in 1982 at Guildhall, London, England. Lady Pindling is second from right.

137. Sir John Templeton, Mrs Pindling, Rev. Billy Graham and H. E. Anthony Roberts, High Commissioner, at Claridge's Hotel in London, early 1980

138. Mrs Pindling talks with television personality Ephraim Zembalist Jr.; on the left is Berkley (Peanuts) Taylor

139. Lady Pindling and HRH the Duke of Edinburgh aboard the Royal Yacht *Britannia*

140. The Pindlings on board the Royal Yacht *Britannia*

141. President Gowan of Nigeria, Mr Lynden Pindling, Mrs Victoria Gowan and Mrs Pindling on a visit to Nassau and Freeport in 1975

142. Sir Clifford Darling, HM the Queen and Lady Pindling at the Commonwealth Heads of Government Meeting in Nassau, October 1985

143. Mrs Pindling with the wife of the Guyanese Ambassador to Great Britain at the Dorchester Hotel, London. *Photo: Howard Glass, Bahamas Information Services*

144. Lady Pindling with the Queen of Swaziland (on her left) at CHOGM in Harare, Zimbabwe, 1991

145. Lady Pindling with Mrs A. N. R. Robinson, Prime Minister of Trinidad and Tobago, at CHOGM in Harare, Zimbabwe, 1991

146. 1980 Templeton Prize Award, 12 May, Buckingham Palace, London

147 HRH the Duke of Edinburgh, Lady Templeton and Mrs Pindling with Professor Ralph Werdell, winner of the 1980 Templeton Prize Award

148. The Pindlings with the Prime Minister of Canada, Pierre Trudeau

149. General Gowan and Mrs Gowan pay a visit to The Bahamas after CHOGM in Jamaica, 1975

150. Lady Pindling and Sir Lynden Pindling with granddaughter Danielle Johnson, daughter of Monique and Daniel Johnson, at Danielle's christening at St Agnes Parish Church, 1999

151. Sir Lynden and Lady Pindling on New Year's Eve, 1999, at the home of Mr and Mrs Franklyn Wilson

152. Dame Marguerite is sworn in as Deputy to the Governor-General by Sir Burton Hall, Chief Justice, October 2006

153. Dame Marguerite Pindling, Deputy to the Governor-General, swears in Mrs Cheryl Albury as Justice to the Supreme Court

154. Dame Marguerite Pindling, Deputy to the Governor-General, receives cookies from the Girl Guides during "Cookie Week", 2006

155. Sir Lynden and Lady Pindling on a cruise to the Mediterranean in 1999 on board the Seven Seas MS *Navigator*

156. Sir Lynden and Lady Pindling with Anglican Archdeacon William Thompson, in late 1999

157. Pastors lay hands on Sir Lynden when he returns from Johns Hopkins Hospital in Baltimore, October 1996, after ten weeks of radiation treatment

158. Dame Marguerite Pindling, Deputy to the Governor-General, with His Excellency Abdullah Ahmed Mohamed A-Murad, Ambassador-Designate of the State of Kuwait and his wife, 5 April 2007

159. Lady Pindling with Gail and Winston Saunders, Professor Rex Nettleford and Ms Minna Israel outside the Dundas Centre for the Performing Arts, about 2004

160. Lady Pindling in the audience at the graduation ceremony at the University of the West Indies (2004) with the Hon. Fred Mitchell, Winston Saunders and Rex Nettleford

161. The Pindling family on Sir Lynden's 70th birthday, 22 March 2000; from left, back row: Danny, Monique and Danielle Johnson, Obi Pindling, Dame Marguerite Pindling, Sir Lynden, Michelle Pindling-Sands, Leslie Pindling, Lauren Sands, Diane Pindling; from left, front row: Andrew Pindling, Holly Sands, Lynden Pindling

162. Lady Pindling with Dame Ivy Dumont and Sir Orville Turnquest attend the swearing-in of the Honourable Arthur D. Hanna as Governor-General at Government House in 2004

163. Dame Marguerite's Investiture at Buckingham Palace, 21 March, 2006

164. Dame Marguerite outside Buckingham Palace with her insignia, 21 March 2006

165. Dame Marguerite with Sir Baltron Bethel and Obi Pindling at a luncheon after her Investiture at Buckingham Palace, 21 March 2006

166. Dame Marguerite shows off her insignia with three of her children (Obi, Leslie and Michelle) outside Buckingham Palace.

167. Dame Marguerite, accompanied by Member of Parliament, the Hon. Fred Mitchell, presents a wreath at Sir Lynden's mausoleum on 10 January 2008

168. Lady Pindling with members of her committee to assist hurricane victims in 1994 present a cheque to the Hon. James Smith, Minister of State in the Ministry of Finance, and the Rt Hon. Perry Christie, Prime Minister

169. Lady Pindling and her granddaughter Holly Sands at the Red Cross Fair, 2004

170. Dame Marguerite with Evangelist Jacqueline Rahming and Dame Ivy Dumont at Church of God of Prophecy, East Street

171. Dame Marguerite, her daughter, Michelle Pindling-Sands and the Hon. Perry Christie (then Prime Minister), present Mr Arthur Hanna with the Lynden Pindling Award for Excellence, 2006

172. Presentations by Dame Marguerite and Michelle Pindling-Sands of the Lynden Pindling Award for Excellence

173. Presentation of the Lynden Pindling Award for Excellence to Mrs Nancy Kelly, 2008

174. Presentation of the Lynden Pindling Award for Excellence to Mr Fred Hazelwood, 2008

175. Presentation of the Lynden Pindling Award for Excellence to Mr Henry Storr, 2008

176. Lady Pindling, Prime Minister Perry Christie and Dame Ivy Dumont attend the funeral of the late Edward St George, Freeport, Grand Bahama

177. Dame Marguerite congratulates Justice Rubie Nottage after she was sworn in as a Justice of the Supreme Court, 28 April 2008

178. Lady Pindling presents Sir Lynden's biography to former President of the United States, Mr Bill Clinton

179. Dame Marguerite with her four children (Leslie, Michelle, Monique and Obi)

180. Dame Marguerite's grandchildren; from left: Lauren and Holly Sands, Danielle and Grace Johnson and Andrew and Lynden Pindling

Christie and his wife Bernadette, long-time friend and political associate the Hon. Arthur Hanna and Bishop Brice Thompson also visited. By late afternoon it was evident that he was dying. His family, close friends and ministers of religion gathered around his bed, singing and praying. He passed away peacefully on Saturday 26 August in the early morning. Lady Pindling admits that the funeral, which was held on Monday 4 September, felt like a large rally – it was not sad: "It was like another rally where people were out there with me showing their support …This gave me strength that I needed … Did I grieve? I guess I did. I said: 'Lord, how am I supposed to manage? How can I live without him?' I know he'd go away but come back – but this was so final." She admits that she had an empty feeling and kept her grief bottled up. She says: "I should have screamed at the funeral."

After his death she tried to keep busy. Immediately following the funeral, she could not concentrate. She thought then: "I don't have a life because I never thought of life without him. He was my life, my world, but I know God has a plan for me." They had been married for 44½ years.

Seven years later, she reflected:

> *It's as fresh as when he died … I think about him constantly. I guess I'm still grieving. Then this feeling takes me in Church … if my faith wasn't strong I don't think we would have gotten through those trials. The things they said about this man named Pindling – the man I know, it cannot be. They kept telling me, Lady Pindling, time will heal this void! It's been seven years now and that void is as fresh as ever. I dream about him – I don't ever see him …*
>
> *When I look back I don't have time to cry, it has given me this satisfaction I never dreamt was possible … he knew what he wanted for his country. He knew nothing about me until he came back from England and I'd never heard of him … When I look back – there's a gospel song that says "When I Look Back Over My Life" – and I think things over, I can truly say that I've been blessed and that testimony is giving thanks to God for what He has done for me – this little island girl; and thank Pindling for exposing me to that particular kind of life and it was no ordinary life – to meet world leaders and their ladies and to sit at the feet of some of them … and so I cry, yes! Cry for joy, I guess. Yes I miss him because it's a lonely life … I have the children but it's not the same. I look back to the beautiful times and that is why I found it difficult to discuss things with certain Bahamian people because it was not on the same level that I had been accustomed to – talking to world leaders' wives … about world*

affairs. Sometimes there was nothing in common to discuss with the people. They were not interested in the things to which I've been accustomed and interested in and I don't have time for all this gossiping.

A year after Sir Lynden's death, the Pindling family established the Sir Lynden Pindling Foundation. Its chairman Michelle Pindling-Sands stated:

The idea really came about during the ten days of mourning after Sir Lynden's passing when people of all walks of life in The Bahamas quite candidly and openly celebrated the life and work of Lynden Pindling. People sent cards, letters, food and flowers, said prayers, held memorial services, a junkanoo parade and a special sitting of the House of Assembly; there were newspaper supplements, news reports and talk shows, people came to visit and expressed warm and sincere wishes all in tribute to a man whom the Prime Minister (the Rt Hon. Hubert Ingraham) of this country has described as the "Architect of the Modern Bahamas". Therefore, in acknowledgement of those sentiments, Sir Lynden's many triumphs and as tribute to our father, we thought it fitting to establish the Sir Lynden Pindling Foundation.

Established as a non-profit company under the Companies Act, 1992, the Foundation's first members comprised Lady Marguerite Pindling (later Dame Marguerite Pindling), L. Obafemi Pindling, Leslie O. Pindling, Michelle M. Pindling-Sands and Monique Pindling-Johnson. Other members of the Board included Mr Edward St George, chairman of the Grand Bahama Port Authority; the Rt. Hon. Arthur D. Hanna, long-time friend, political colleague and a founding father of the Commonwealth of The Bahamas; Lady Patricia Isaacs, a school friend of Sir Lynden; Professor Rex Nettleford, then Vice-Chancellor of the University of the West Indies; Mr Norman Solomon, President of The Solomon Group of Companies; Dr William Thompson, President of The Bahamas National Baptist Convention; and Mr Carlton Williams, businessman. Also established was an advisory board which gave direction on policy and management of the Foundation. Members included Winston V. Saunders, attorney at law and cultural activist, and Dr Keva M. Bethel, former Principal and President of the College of The Bahamas.

As Michelle Pindling-Sands stated at the launch of the Foundation:

The primary object and purpose ... is to promote the legacy of Sir Lynden Pindling by developing programmes and projects for the benefit of the people of The Bahamas which are geared to enhance national pride, social responsibility, historical and environmental awareness and preservation, cultural creativity and socially constructive recreation, mutual respect, understanding, positive interaction and social concord enhancing self-sufficiency, positive and healthy self-expression, community upliftment, and industry.

At its establishment, the Foundation had as a long-term goal the acquisition of land on which it would "build or cause to have built a library or historical museum or educational center or institute" similar to presidential libraries in the United States. It was envisaged at the time that the planned facility could house historical papers of the Pindling years and display gifts given to the late Prime Minister and also personal memorabilia of Sir Lynden.

This idea was modified later. The College of The Bahamas approached the Foundation, asking it to lend its support to a special programme to celebrate the birthday of Sir Lynden "with a view to raising funds to create an endowment fund at the College of The Bahamas in the name of Sir Lynden". The Foundation has to date pledged $300,000 to the College of The Bahamas to assist with its new library, from funds raised from six Legacy Balls held between 2000 and 2006.

The Foundation and the College of The Bahamas plan to incorporate a space in the new library in which to exhibit Sir Lynden's memorabilia, similar to the display in the St Augustine Library, University of the West Indies, in Trinidad which commemorates the life of former Prime Minister and scholar Eric Williams.

Besides the donation to the College of The Bahamas, the Foundation also donated 11 computers to the South Andros High School.

Another fund-raising event begun by the Sir Lynden Pindling Foundation was the prayer breakfasts which celebrated Sir Lynden's legacy, gave thanks for his life and work and honoured ministers who "provided steadfast spiritual leadership for our Country, and who served as personal spiritual advisors to him". In March 2003 the first one was held and ten ministers – Pastor Clarke, Mother Colebrooke, Bishop Dawkins, Rev. Green, Rev. Stewart, Rev. Stubbs, Bishop Thompson, Rev. Burns, Rev. Neely and Rev. Rolle – were honoured for "prayers and Christian counsel that they provided to Sir Lynden during his political career". Prayer breakfasts were also held in 2004, 2005 and 2006. About 400 people attended the events according to Dame Marguerite, mostly "die-hard" PLPs and church people.

A memorial lecture series, in association with the College of The Bahamas, to be held each March, began in 2001. The Hon. Paul Adderley, former Attorney-General, Minister of Foreign Affairs, Minister of Education and Minister of Finance gave the first lecture to a large crowd at the Dundas Centre for the Performing Arts. The informative lecture, entitled "From Pompey to Pindling", gave insight into black leadership from the nineteenth century to modern times. The Hon. George Mackey, former Minister in the Pindling Cabinet and Member of Parliament for Fox Hill, delivered the second, followed by Fred Mitchell, whose topic was "What It Means to be Bahamian". Patricia Glinton Meicholas, author and a vice-president at the College of The Bahamas, was the first woman to give the lecture in 2005, after a year's hiatus. On 22 March, Sir Lynden's birthday, she spoke on the provoking topic "32 past 73: Time to assess who we were, who we are and who we can become". A week later, Professor Rex Nettleford, former Vice-Chancellor of the University of the West Indies and member of the Board of the Sir Lynden Pindling Foundation, examined "Pindling's Far-reaching Vision for Culture in Development".

Both Meicholas' and Nettleford's talks were stimulating and well attended. Michelle Pindling-Sands reminded Bahamians that as her "father once observed, we forget often too quickly, that ours is a brilliant legacy and a rich culture – something that we should hold on to". She continued: "I can think of no better way to celebrate the 75th anniversary of his birth than to spend two evenings enriching our minds and reminding ourselves of that brilliant legacy and rich culture with what promise to be fascinating presentations by Patricia Glinton Meicholas and Professor Nettleford."

The 2007 lecture, entitled "Global Caribbean Trade and Labour: Imperatives of Bahamian Economic Problems", was given by Dr Eugene Newry.

Lady Pindling, after the 2002 election which was won by the PLP, again assisted the Red Cross and was appointed co-chairman along with Mrs Pauline Allen of the Fair Committee. She and Mrs Allen organized four fairs which were successful, especially when the venue was returned to the grounds of Government House.

Another charity in which Lady Pindling participated was the Ranfurly Home for Children. She supported the Home by selling tickets on Bay Street at the start-up of the campaign. She boldly called several important people, including Deputy Prime Minister, the Hon. Brent Symonette: "DPM; my name is Marguerite Pindling calling to ask for assistance for the Ranfurly Home for Children. I want your support on Bay Street." Not surprisingly, Brent Symonette went to Bay Street and bought $500 worth of tickets from Dame Marguerite. Nancy Kelly, whom she had worked with on the Hurricane Committee, bought $500 worth of tickets and so did the Hon. Neville Wisdom.

Nova Scotia Bank gave a sizeable donation. It was obvious that people bought tickets because Dame Marguerite was there. One lady was delighted to see her as she had been longing to thank her for baby clothes that Dame Marguerite had given her. The "children" for whom the clothes were given were now grown, married and had children of their own. In two hours Dame Marguerite raised $7,900 and felt very pleased with her accomplishment.

Perhaps one of the highlights in her career and life was the bestowal on her of the DCMG, Dame Commander of the Most Distinguished Order of Saint Michael and Saint George, by Queen Elizabeth II. Named in the Queen's New Year's Honours list for 2007 along with Sir Garet "Tiger" Finlayson and Sir Baltron Bethel who received knighthoods, Dame Marguerite was honoured for service to politics, community development and charitable work. She had worked in public life for 50 years from 1956 and was the only living spouse of the freedom fighters who was still active. She was gratified by the honour but she felt "the country should know about it". She admitted that she made her feelings known to the Governor-General, the Hon. A. D. Hanna.

Another high point in her life was in October 2006, when she was sworn in as Deputy to the Governor-General on a rainy Saturday morning. About 50 of her political friends and her children were there. They, especially Monique, wished her to stay active.

An amusing incident occurred at her first official engagement as Deputy to the Governor-General. She had to deliver a speech at a ceremony sponsored by the Ministry of Agriculture at Government House. She almost panicked when in the middle of her speech, the pages were stuck together. Fortunately, her training in the Dale Carnegie course had taught her well. She had focused on Reverend Evans from her home island of Andros and while she was trying to get the pages unstuck she ad libbed, addressing Rev. Evans and congratulating Andros for being honoured this evening, and no one in the audience knew what had occurred.

During her stint as Deputy to the Governor-General which lasted intermittently for one year, she attended in an official capacity a service at her own parish church, St Agnes and another one at Abundant Life Church. She also swore in Cheryl Albury as an Acting Justice of the Supreme Court, cut a ribbon to open the computer room at Kingsway Academy, officiated at the Public Service Union banquet and received cookies from the Bahamas Girl Guides during their special week. She was honoured to receive the Credentials of the Kuwaiti Ambassador to The Bahamas – "That was an exciting one and I was coached by Andrew McKinney and he told me I did well."

A social highlight of her tenure was, after encouragement from Government House staff, the hosting of a dinner at Government House.

She invited politicians, close friends including Rubie and Kendal Nottage, Rosemarie Thompson, Lady Isaacs, Cypriana and Sean McWeeney, Alice McKenzie, Al Collie, Basil Sands and Mrs Roberta Sands, Reno Brown and Mary, his wife, and Winston and Gail Saunders. The Prime Minister, the Rt Hon. Perry Christie and his wife Bernadette attended, as did ministers in his Cabinet, Neville Wisdom, the Hon. Alfred Gray and Mrs Gray. Other government officials included Sir Burton Hall, Chief Justice, and Lady Hall. Religious figures, including Fr. Rodney Burrows and Barbara Burrows and Rev. Roach and Mrs Roach also attended the dinner.

Dame Marguerite admits that she felt "let down" by the 2007 general election, but that she expected it. She states:

> The feeling wasn't there. I knew we were going to lose. That election feeling – that PLP feeling wasn't there.... You could tell from the people's behaviour. It wasn't the PLP campaign – you don't change in mid-stream – you're fighting an election, that's political war.... Now don't change your pattern of campaigning and holding rallies like that – introducing new things.... You use what you know is made to win the game. And the people – something was missing – it wasn't there. The Family Islands stuck with us.... It wasn't the same – it wasn't elections as I know them to be. I was not involved actually ...

After the FNM victory, Dame Marguerite's social life was less active, but she continued to attend some public functions. Her attention as usual was directed towards her children and their families, and her extended family. She continued cooking for the family on Sundays and caring for the grandchildren when called upon, especially on Saturday. She recalled that one Sunday, during a period when the automatic gate to her property was not functioning, a former beauty salon operator drove up to the house, rang the doorbell and asked for some lunch. Of course, she complied.

On Thursday 11 October 2007 Dame Marguerite woke with a terrible pain in her abdomen and began vomiting. Her daughter Monique quickly reacted and took her to the Princess Margaret Hospital. Her doctors, Conville Brown and Dwayne Sands, admitted her to the intensive care unit of the PMH and treated her for pancreatitis. Visitors were limited to immediate family. She remained in a serious condition for over a week and was not moved from the intensive care unit to a regular room in the private surgical ward until Monday 22 October. When restrictions were relaxed hordes of friends and acquaintances including Prime Minister Ingraham and former Prime Minister Perry Christie, paid visits to Dame Marguerite. The numbers of well-wishers were so numerous, doctors were forced to reinstate the "No Visitors" rule. Newspapers continued to issue reports on Dame Marguerite's progress.

Discharged on Tuesday 30 October, Dame Marguerite made a rapid recovery with the help of her family and was soon feeling energetic again. She recalled that the hospital staff were excellent except perhaps for a few "bad apples" on the nursing staff. She highly commended Drs Dwayne Sands, Conville Brown and Perry Gomez who attended her. She boasted that she kept the nurses and hospital staff "on their toes" and tutored them on how to "speak to people" and about good manners.

11
Her Children Speak

Dame Marguerite and Sir Lynden's children, Obafemi (Obi), Leslie, Michelle and Monique are delightful human beings and speak with passion and pride about their mother and father. Obi, Leslie and Michelle were born before Majority Rule (1967) in a four-year period between February 1959 and November 1962. Monique, the youngest child, born after the Progressive Liberal Party came to power, did not experience what it was like to be a child of the Leader of the Opposition.

The Pindling children describe their upbringing as typically Bahamian. All of them, but especially Obi, Leslie and Michelle, state that their mother was "the most strict mother that any child could have ... she believed in spare the rod and spoil the child. We grew up under that banner and she never once hesitated to beat with whatever she could find. Her favourite 'weapon' was a switch and it could sting."

A strict disciplinarian, Dame Marguerite did not hesitate to punish her children when they misbehaved. Leslie remembers most about the beatings as he admits he was the cause of most of them and that he got most of it.

Leslie states that they were not allowed to chew gum, to play cards, dominoes or even Monopoly. He says even to this day he does not chew gum or play cards. That was the way she was. She had her rules and very simple laws: you had to come straight home and always to be home before dark. She did not like them "keeping company" and going to parties. However, they were allowed to play with children – friends they had in the neighbourhood. These included the children of L. B. Johnson, Percy Campbell, Percy Munnings, Robert Bartlett and Felix Seymour. They played the usual childhood games such as marbles and hop-scotch; they skated, and rode bicycles on Soldier Road which in those days had little traffic.

One incident that Obi, Leslie and Michelle, whose ages then ranged between seven and ten, remember, is the day they attended a cook-out at Holy Cross Church. They had their parents' permission but their mistake was that they stayed too long. Michelle relates that their mother:

> *summoned up the whole neighbourhood of children to go and find us and when they did, they said, "Boy, you're in trouble. Your mummy looking for you and she say to come home. You're going*

to get beating." Then the whole gang of kids walked up with us from the Holy Cross Church to our home.

When they arrived home, their mother was on the telephone and they tried to sneak past her, but she finished her call and "came at us with the switch asking where had we been, beating with every word.... She whipped and whipped, told us to take a bath and whipped us even in the tub." Michelle says, "it was a royal beating", one she would never forget. She adds that they were never injured, never hit in the head or bruised. The beating was mainly on the legs and arms and the switch stung.

Dame Marguerite did most of the beating, as her husband was very busy running the country. However, occasionally, especially on a Sunday afternoon, when their parents were resting and the children were thought to be napping, they misbehaved and received a beating with a thin narrow brown belt from their father.

Leslie believes that children today need a "good cut skin" and that his mother would be a good one to teach them. Ironically, Dame Marguerite chided Leslie when he was about to hit one of her grandchildren. He was surprised at "the Queen of Beating" shouting at him: "Don't touch my grandchildren." Monique, who was five years younger than Michelle, never remembers being disciplined or getting beaten. An exception was the unsuccessful attempt by her mother when Monique was 14. Monique admits that she did not remember her mother in a "Mother role". She was not the typical mummy as far as homework or Parent Teachers' Association meetings were concerned. If Dame Marguerite visited her school, it was usually in an official capacity.

Although the children had normal childhoods, they realized fairly early in their lives that their parents were important. But as Michelle comments, "it was more as a result of people's reaction to me as opposed to me thinking my parents were important people. Even now, you would be told 'you is Pindling daughter'. Someone would recognize you and make a comment like that." Comments were not always complimentary. Even in the early years of school, at Queen's College, where Michelle started in reception, she was "aware of something", but as she moved up in the school she encountered it more from her teachers, and says, "My children are experiencing it now when teachers find out that they are grandchildren of Lynden and Marguerite Pindling." Her years at Queen's College were good ones – she was just another student. She, Obi, Leslie and Monique agree that "Mummy and Daddy never, ever, ever, made us feel that we were any more special, any more important, or even different from the other children ... but we were different." Take transportation, for example. Their father became Premier in 1967 when Michelle was five, and Prime Minister two years later. Her parents were chauffeured on his becoming Premier so they had no reason to drive.

When they first attended Queen's College they were taken to school by their neighbour Charmaine Johnson, but at some point the police driver began taking them. Obi, however, remembers their parents driving. One of his earliest memories is the frequent trips to the airport, with their mother driving, to pick up their father. However, this was short-lived, and the children admit that it was perhaps unusual that their parents did not drive. Besides not coming to PTA meetings, they rarely came to see them in school plays or the like. Later, when Michelle was in High School, she remembers her mother coming to see her perform in the dance section of the National Arts Festival. Michelle studied ballet for 12 years. She admits that her mother's attendance was two-fold, to see her and to present awards, one of which she won. The children do not remember their mother or father assisting them with their homework. Not only were they very busy, Obi observes, but his mother had had a limited education. Fortunately, they were all good students and did well in school.

Michelle recalls that birthdays were not usually celebrated. On her birthdays, she says, "Daddy would come into my bedroom, wish me a happy birthday, kiss me on my forehead and off he went. That's how I remember many of my birthdays. I don't remember parties ... and I don't feel I missed out on anything ... although they were not home a lot." There were staff who looked after them. They were never alone. In the very early days when their parents had a function, Obi, Leslie and Michelle were looked after by their Pindling grandparents.

The Pindling children were never put in the spotlight by their parents, who thought the children were not to be treated any differently or any more favourably than anyone else. For example, they were not allowed to use their father's Bahamasair pass, and had to stand in line like everyone else. Michelle's friends chide her today for not taking advantage of her name and heritage. She cannot remember ever throwing her weight around and asking "Do you know who I am?" Of course, if she travelled with her parents, it was different as they naturally received special treatment. Monique recalls that her friends also remind her and her siblings of their importance but chide them for treating it so lightly. "They say we all act as if it's nothing, but to us it's nothing." Often they would see their mother scrubbing the floor, as if no one could scrub it the way she wanted it. She also ironed all the shirts her husband wore and made sure all his clothes were laid out on the bed. She organized Sir Lynden and the household, as many people were in and out of their home.

Obi remembers their mother taking them to church, first attending St Agnes and later Holy Cross when they moved to Soldier Road. Obi recalls that Holy Cross began in Father Pestaina's driveway on Robinson Road.

The Pindlings, the Percy Campbells, the L. B. Johnsons, the Felix Seymours and the Bartletts families were among the first members of the congregation of Holy Cross Anglican Church.

In the political arena, he speaks of the curried-goat parties, PLP fund-raisers, held at their Soldier Road home, organized by their mother, Mrs Beverley Whitfield, Mrs Beryl Hanna, Mrs Vernice Cooper, Ms Effie Walkes and others. Dame Marguerite was very involved with the PLP Women's Branch.

Obi agrees with his siblings that his parents never tried to make them feel any different from other children, and their parents behaved no differently from their friends' parents. He fondly remembers his mother cooking and eating boiled crab and dough and his father sucking fish bones dry. Obi states: "We grew up as ordinary children in an ordinary Bahamian home." Michelle admits, though, that after 1967 her father and mother were more in the public eye. Dame Marguerite was extremely supportive of Sir Lynden and usually accompanied him and became a public figure in her own right. But she remained a good housewife and a devoted mother and grandmother. She maintained a close relationship with her children from childhood to adulthood.

Obi recalls that the only "absolute negative" in being a Pindling, a PLP or a black child was when at the age of eight, he was moved from St Anne's Primary School, a predominantly black school, to Grade 4 of Queen's College, a predominantly white school, in September 1967. He recounts:

> *At the end of the first week, four big white boys from Grade 6 held me down and plastered me with UBP (United Bahamian Party – then the opposition political party) stickers from head to toe. I was rescued by Robert Archer who now owns Archer's Nursery in Chippingham. Robert remains my friend and although we do not see each other often, we share that camaraderie.*

Besides that experience, there were no other problems either racial or political, in spite of the fact that the majority of his classmates and in fact most of the students were white.

Three years later, Obi transferred to the Government High School (GHS) although he wished to stay at Queen's College. His father chose the predominantly black school where he graduated in the class of 1975. He said that although he did not understand why his father moved him, his experience at Government High in the 1970s, was the "best thing that happened to him". He still has an unbelievable bond with his classmates. Obi describes the Government High at the time as a private school attended by children who had all passed the common entrance examinations, from ordinary Bahamian families. "It was an amazing experience. We lived ordinary lives"; and even now he is still bonded with his Soldier Road childhood friends: "When I think of my childhood, I think of Soldier Road and the Government High School."

Throughout their lives, the children shared a closeness with their parents. Sir Lynden took Obi to London after Government High and a year of Grade 13 at Trinity College School in Port Hope, Ontario, Canada. He attended the University of Sussex in Brighton from the age of 17 and became a lawyer. His mother, who accompanied Michelle to Le Rosey school near Geneva in Switzerland, visited them often, especially if they needed her support. For instance, as Michelle recalls, she told her mother that a girl had been expelled from Le Rosey for using drugs.

> *Mummy found herself on the plane to Geneva to come to the school to let people there know that her child doesn't get mixed up in that sort of thing, in case they are looking for someone to blame. It was not her daughter. Yes, I remember she came up for that. It's interesting that it was then she did the school visits. While we were home, I don't recall my parents visiting school.*

Obi recounts an amusing story of how surprised his mother was on receiving his first letter while he was at school in Canada. He had always refused to speak the Queen's English:

> *I always spoke Bahamian dialect from a child; that was always my mother's pet peeve with me: "Boy when you going to speak properly?"*
>
> *"Mummy, I know how to speak properly. I choose not to speak it".*
>
> *Mummy said, "You are going off to school [in Canada] now and I know you're going to speak properly when you go."*
>
> *So I go off to Canada and I write my first letter home to my parents. Mummy called me:*
>
> *Mummy: Hi, I just got your letter.*
> *Obi: It reach there already?*
> *Mummy: Who wrote it? The grammar, the English, is perfect!*
> *Obi: What do you mean who wrote it? Can't you see it's in my handwriting?*
> *Mummy: But the grammar, the English, is perfect!*

Obi: I wrote it. Mummy, when you go into exams, you can't talk, you supposed to write. I can write the Queen's English.

Mummy: But the English is perfect!

Obi: I have been telling you all the time that I know English; I just refuse to speak it. You can thank Mrs [Anatol] Rodgers, Dr [Keva] Bethel, Mrs Marjorie Jones and Ms Felicity Johnson, all of them [former GHS teachers] for my English.

I came back from Canada after that one year as Bahamian as I gon'.

When Obi was leaving for England to attend university his mother said "You only had one year in Canada, you are going to England now. I know you will come back speaking proper English." Much to her dismay, nothing changed. Obi says that what is so ironic is that his mother now often asks him to assist her with her speeches.

Leslie relates a story of how he discovered the importance of his parents. He also attended Queen's College and admits he was not doing well there. One day he returned home and as he came down the hall in their home at Long Bay, on passing the living room, he saw all his teachers discussing his future with his parents. "That made you think, as a little boy." He was then about 12 or 13. Normally parents would visit the school, but this was the opposite. He learned of their decision and his fate by listening over the intercom. He would attend boarding school where he would be taught discipline and receive a good education. In hindsight, he thinks this was the best decision. At the time, he had no choice and attended Trinity College School (TCS) in Ontario, Canada.

Leslie also recalls a time when he was playing soccer at Trinity College, and all of a sudden a helicopter landed and his father stepped off to make a brief visit. Leslie marvels at how quickly he was accepted at Trust House Forte. His father spoke with Lord Forte on a Friday and on the Monday he was in as a student of Trust House Forte.

Monique notes that her mother was very upset when Leslie left. She admits that her mother "dotes on Leslie". Monique thinks that this stems from the fact that Leslie did not get on so well with his grandfather as Obi did, and perhaps her feelings toward Leslie compensated for this.

Leslie and Monique, who are very close, agree that there was always "a presence of love" in the family; even though their father was often absent, they had quality time together, usually at their lunchtime gatherings and on their Family Island trips. Their father usually took them on local trips to Andros where the older children spent time every summer with their grandmother (Mrs McKenzie). There they used the hand pumps and outside toilet and ate fish, conch, coco plums, scarlet plums, cassava and other local foods and went to the well down the road to get water. They also visited Exuma, especially at regatta time. When travelling with their parents, they had to attend every ceremony and event, usually at the insistence of their mother who was very sensitive to their appearance and behaviour in public. They admit they "couldn't do anything" because of who their parents were.

Monique and her siblings agree that their mother was "a great mother ... and could cook ... she is a great cook. Her stew fish is the best in the world. She puts okra in stew fish ... and coconut milk in baked bone fish. We rarely ate out at restaurants ... you know, you can get a better meal at home ... you're so used to having coconut milk in your peas and rice". Such food helped to keep them healthy. In fact Lynden and Marguerite Pindling were very healthy until much later in life.

As stated previously, Dame Marguerite was a "politician". Michelle recalls her mother's loyalty to her father. She watched his back and was very protective of him. People realized that in order to get to Prime Minister Pindling, they had to go through Dame Marguerite. She was an unofficial adviser to her husband and was politically savvy. Michelle states: "Daddy's survival politically had a lot to do with Mummy." She was a strong character, protector and friend to her husband. Michelle describes Dame Marguerite as the "strongest woman I know ... stronger than the Iron Lady [Mrs Thatcher]". She did not tolerate weakness, but at the same time she was a kind person.

Obi relates:

> My mother had this amazing knack to fit in. Daddy spent his early political life trying to bring Majority Rule to the Country, but a part of the struggle was the Women's Suffrage Movement. My mother was part of that and I can vividly recall seeing Mummy and Mrs Hanna making noise and raising hell on Bay Street. She learned on the job. The wives of the politicians were all very close ... my mother, Mrs Hanna, Mrs Wallace Whitfield, Mrs Jeffrey Thompson; Mummy would often take us to visit the different families. These included the families of Carl Francis, Arthur Hanna and Curtis Macmillan."

Many of the children of the "freedom fighters" are still close – there is a bond in spite of the nasty political fights. Obi is close to Tommy Turnquest and Michelle Turnquest Fields, and Brendon, Dion and Chantal Foulkes

Bethel. "As you get older, you realize that politics is just a game.... I wish something could happen in this country, as the general electorate does not realize that even the politicians themselves are close friends, but the public only see the rancour, the arguments and fighting during the campaign and that's what they do for political reasons."

Michelle remembers her mother saying on more than one occasion: "If I was Prime Minister I would ..."; Sir Lynden would answer: "That's why I am." Dame Marguerite could not put up with disloyalty and according to Michelle, "She had a political view on everything." She says that her mother was fiercely independent and advised Michelle "not to depend on anyone to do anything for you – do it yourself."

Obi "hates politics" and was deeply affected by the criticisms levelled at his father, especially those aired on NBC in 1983 which led to the Commission of Inquiry into drug smuggling in The Bahamas. Even before that crisis, he was sensitive to criticism of his parents. He thinks that he was the most sensitive of the four children and he states that he would never subject himself or his family to a political career.

He is still amazed at the talk about all the drug money that his father was said to have received and the so called "Swiss accounts". People are not aware that:

> after he [Sir Lynden] lost the election in 1992 and went into private life, the only income beside his salary as Leader of the Opposition and as a Member of Parliament that he had was what I was paying him as a salary here, and I would be here trying to help him make financial ends meet ... I always say if he had those accounts when he died, I would have been on the first flight to Geneva to collect mine as heir.

Obi was similarly deeply affected in 1983 when the NBC story broke of the dynamite explosion on the dock in Marsh Harbour, Abaco, near where Sir Lynden was speaking. Obi saw it as an attempt on his father's life. He asked his father if being a public figure was worth it. Sir Lynden replied: "This is the path I chose and in this business you have to learn to have a thick skin." Obi admits how hurt he was as a son by the various accusations. He could only imagine how his mother was affected as Sir Lynden's wife. Sir Lynden always said, "It comes with the territory", and "I always said to myself, that's one territory I don't want anything to do with."

Obi wonders how his parents did it as "you know, the electorate is not always kind." He says that he has friends on both sides of the political divide. He asked an FNM friend whom he had advised against a political career, who is now [2008] serving in the FNM Cabinet, how was he faring.

The reply was, "Boy, Obi, I should have listened to you... If I had known then what I know now, it is a thankless job. You can never do enough." Obi adds that his father has been dead for seven years and he is still being "cussed" on the talk shows, "but this is one Pindling they don't have to worry about getting into politics."

Notwithstanding, Obi admits that the people who are still critical of his father are in the minority. He says:

> I have heard some of my father's bitterest political enemies over the years say such complimentary things about him publicly. I've heard hard-core FNMs say complimentary things about him... The country would not be where it is today, were it not for your dad ... so at the end of the day, the majority of people appreciate what was done, but to hear one person criticize him still hurts. I still lead an ordinary life ... even when Daddy was Prime Minister, I never liked the attention of being the child of the Prime Minister ... I always shied away from public life.

Leslie and Monique agree with Obi that some of Sir Lynden's political enemies were genuinely fond of him. Norman Solomon cried over Sir Lynden at home when he was dying. William Saunders, owner of Majestic Tours, is now a professional colleague of Leslie's. Hubert Ingraham, Prime Minister from 1992 to 2002 and re-elected in 2007, spoke in glowing terms of Sir Lynden at his funeral. Monique thinks that Mr Ingraham had a soft spot for her father, but was "peeved" because he was fired.

Michelle remarks on the difficult times, the criticisms and the lives of the Pindling children, especially after the defeat of the Progressive Liberal Party in 1992. She comments on the attitudes of some Bahamians towards them:

> [Bahamians are now] coming out of Law School from UWI, the United Kingdom and the Eugene Dupuch Law School in droves, but that's okay, it's not a big deal for anyone to go and study law in the UK or for kids to go off to boarding school, but when Pindling's kids did it, it was wrong, they should not have it, and I am a little resentful, to say that I am unscathed would be untrue ... and I need to get beyond that ... I shall let it go, but I won't forget it.

She emphasizes that she was "proud of my mother and proud of my father and proud of the way they brought us up.... When he died, I remember saying to Mummy, it's just us now, we have to depend on us to get us through this. So said, so done."

She recalls that in 1992 when the PLP lost after being in power for 25 years, and when Sir Lynden died, "'the 'friends' disappeared, the phone stopped ringing, except for the real friends, and life became very different." It was not only painful for Michelle, but a very distressing experience for her mother, who "may not admit it, but is so aware of the fight, the contribution that they made, and quite frankly the life that Bahamians now enjoy is what they were fighting for." Michelle admits that she may be a bit cynical at times, as when she hears people complain and state what their rights are, she sits back and smiles because they take it all for granted and are not aware of the process – how this came about. However, she thinks that "one day, the contribution of Marguerite and Lynden Pindling, will really, really be appreciated." In fact, she admits that it is happening already:

> *People are beginning to see what he was about in nation-building and the same thing has already happened with Mummy; she can go anywhere, any function, and she will be warmly greeted by persons of all political persuasion and I believe she is beginning to see it come back to her and that's something she needs to be proud of. We couldn't be more proud. They gave us a social upbringing, manners was a very strong thing, that was just a given ...*

This was an important legacy and Michelle says she is trying to do the same thing with her children, but admits that children today are different. She never uses the switch' though, but is strict and disciplines them and says "It's the mummy in me. Monique and I joke, the Marguerite in me came out ... Marguerite is in me, in all of us, and Lynden is in all of us but especially Marguerite, the determination, sometimes to a fault ... that unbending determination. That's the influence in my life."

Michelle also speaks of her own and her mother's strength and determination during her (Michelle's) bout with breast cancer:

> *All I have ever known is fight, don't give up and there was never any doubt in my mind that I was going to cope, deal, get through and I would say in large part, that's Mummy – that strength and determination. There were prayers but you have to have that inner strength, the will to fight it ... I knew no other way – that's Mummy. There was no question about it ... in fact it was more difficult and painful, to tell Mummy about it as we were rarely ill.*

Dame Marguerite not only dealt with the bad news, she actively supported Michelle during her illness. She accompanied her during her consultations at the Johns Hopkins University Hospital:

She handled it very well and together we were good. I knew that I had to be strong just as during the Commission of Inquiry into drugs. Mummy never showed us a weak side ... she always put up a very strong front and I know I did that with the breast cancer and my children. I knew that I could not at any time let Lauren and Holly see for a minute that I would be worried or afraid, then they would be worried and afraid. I needed them to keep on keeping on, which they managed to do.

She admits that she only slipped once after a bad bout of chemotherapy. When the children left for school she was in bed and when Holly came home from school and saw her still there, she had "the look on her face and asked if I was sick". Michelle was determined after that to keep up a strong front. The days that she had chemotherapy when they were at school, whatever her feelings, she was always up and dressed. Holly's attitude was absolutely different. She spoke to her mother and went about her business. "That again was Mummy. Even when things were at their lowest, and we have had some low times, this country does not know the half of what we have been through, especially on a personal level, but it is that strength that Mummy has. That commercial says 'Never let them see you sweat.'"

Another slogan was written on a plaque hanging in their kitchen in Skyline Drive: "Don't let the bastards get you down." Those were watchwords for her. Michelle says that she knows that she (Michelle) lived those words but would only admit her true feelings to her very close friends. The general public would never know. She attributes her inner strength to her mother and although she admits it was not always a good thing, when she needed it, "it was there for me to draw on."

Leslie and Monique also speak about their mother's determination and political savvy. Leslie comments that some people, even those in the PLP, looked down on his mother because she had no college degree. This attitude increased her determination to prove them wrong. She learned the ways of politics very quickly and was the "fire" behind her husband. Leslie sees his mother as a more political beast than his father. She had a fighting spirit. She was hell bent on proving people wrong and was good for him. But he thinks that the people of The Bahamas loved Lynden and Marguerite Pindling. Monique says that even after losing power her mother was still revered. "I hope that my parents instilled in people of the country – ain't no glamour or glitz, it's hard work; you have to represent your people ... if Mummy and Daddy had not given their all, where would we be?" They showed how things should be done and valued standards such as punctuality.

All the children were also proud of their mother's looks, style and elegance.

Michelle recalls that her mother emulated Jackie Kennedy. She even wore the goggle sunglasses which were then in vogue. After Jackie Kennedy left public life, Dame Marguerite followed the Royal Family, mostly the Queen and Princess Diana. When Dame Marguerite visited her at "Le Rosey":

> it was not so much that she was wife of the Prime Minister, but it was how Mummy presented and she was stunning. As you could imagine, Mummy arrived at the school, and she was wearing at the time – I guess this may not be politically correct – but she was wearing a full-length dark mink coat and she wore a felt hat with a feather, the feather stood off about two feet from the hat. But when she stepped out of the car, she was so, so, elegant. People at that school – at "Le Rosey" everyone's parents are elegant, everybody's parents wear mink coats – so it was not unusual, but it was my mother who could look so sharp, so stunning, so elegant, that everyone did stop and take notice.

Michelle at the age of 16 was the only black girl at "Le Rosey" at the time. Shirley Bassey had a son at the school whose name was Mark Novac; he was younger and probably the only black boy. Michelle believes that the people at the school did not expect the image that her mother presented.

> About my mother, I will say, full kudos for the way she presents, because she does present, no matter what the occasion, Mummy is always very, very sharp and always very elegant and poised.
>
> I keep saying to her, this barefoot gal from Andros, with her high top tennis, and look at her now and it reminds me as I say that, I felt exactly that same way at Buckingham Palace to think that my mother, who, as she would say, had no high school education, just primary education, could be so elegant and so poised to receive her Damehood. Even she said afterwards at the luncheon, who would have thought, that someone so educationally limited from Long Bay Cays, Andros, with the background that she had ... to think that she rose to that level, to that stature. I was really proud.

Michelle sat between Obi and Leslie in the ballroom at Buckingham Palace and she was nudging them, saying: "'Look at Mummy' and she was there standing alone in the distance, in the doorway waiting for her name to be called, and the three of us said, 'Boy, Daddy should have been here because he would have been so, so, proud' ... He would have said something like 'Look at the old girl'. We were so proud of her. The Queen remembered her and they had a real conversation." Michelle says that her mother leaves her mark indelibly on people. The honour and recognition of her contribution was individual and separate from Sir Lynden's. She earned it in her own right.

All the children were devastated and scared when Dame Marguerite became seriously ill with pancreatitis in 2007. As Obi reflects, his parents were rarely ill, and his mother was a tower of strength. He was disturbed. It was a shock to all the children to see their mother so gravely ill. Obi says:

> *We grew up in a family where neither of our parents were ever sick, never sick. I don't remember seeing my mother or father with a flu, a cold maybe, but never a flu when they had to be bedridden ... and so after she came down with her illness and had to be admitted, and the doctors ... told us how serious it was, I remember looking at Michelle, Leslie and Monique and saying "You'd think Mummy and Daddy could stop this foolishness, they go from being perfectly healthy, to getting these debilitating illnesses from which they can die." It stunned all of us, because she had been a tower of strength in the house, you could never get her to sit down, she was always cleaning this or cooking that or rearranging that, being out in the garden ... To see her in the state that she was, was unbelievable, devastating ... Mummy had been a tower of strength when things were tough when people were out there saying all those things about Daddy, she was in there, trying to keep us strong ... she probably might have been suffering but did not show us.*

Obi comments on the "outpouring of support and sympathy" that he received:

> *Everywhere I went in this country, I could not believe it. There's a certain newspaper that paints Mummy in an image that makes her appear to be almost evil, overbearing and dictatorial, which is not her.... It seems that she is so well loved (as Sir Lynden is by many) in this country. It really was a national outpouring. I didn't realize that people loved her to that extent. I knew they thought highly of her.*

Michelle also reminisces:

> *When she became ill, it almost felt as if there was a hush that came over the island [of New Providence]. "Oh, my God, Lady Pindling sick, she's in the hospital!" I think she represents or holds*

> *a place of prominence in this country among all Bahamians and I think everyone, but everyone, stopped in their tracks when they heard she was taken to hospital, and I don't think that would happen for someone who has not made a mark on the country, and I don't think it is a political mark or anything. She has definitely made a place for herself in this country and I think people recognize that. And everywhere I go, it doesn't matter if I know or don't know the person, everyone will ask "How's your mother?" And even before she was ill, since Daddy's passing people asked: "How is your mother?" She's very well respected in all circles in this country and you know, I have to say, I admire her ... Mummy has her limitations, but ... she has excelled in areas that other people only aspire to reach. She's not an academic, she never professed, never tried to be ... just her nature, her instinct, her leadership skills, her political skills, her fighting skills, all of that.*

Suzanne Black, who asked about Dame Marguerite, said to Michelle, 'Your mother has what I would call an indomitable spirit." Michelle reflects: "But you know, Mummy does have an indomitable spirit. When people see her, when she's out, people think 'Oh, Lady Pindling's here' ... she lifts the occasion ... the room lights up and that transcends politics."

The respect and affection held for Dame Marguerite was evident when Prime Minister Hubert Ingraham visited her in hospital during her illness. Michelle was present. She recalls:

> *There is no doubt in my mind from the expression on his face and his whole demeanour, he recognized that he was in the presence of someone very special and someone very important. Hubert Ingraham was very quiet, very respectful, very demure. He was extremely caring and sensitive. I just remember being struck by that gentle demeanour that he exhibited in the intensive care unit that day. She even commands his respect ... he thought as Leader of the country that was something he ought to do, something made him find himself at her side, she really commands and demands respect from top to the bottom.*

Obi concurs that Hubert Ingraham was sincerely moved when he visited Dame Marguerite in hospital and said "She'll always be my girl". Obi believes that Hubert Ingraham had a love for both his parents, as he really did not have to say "the things he said about Daddy at his funeral". "The way he was with mummy in the hospital and the way he spoke about Daddy at the funeral" made Obi change his general attitude towards him. "The person we saw in public was the politician and he's got his style ... and you can't please everybody ... we saw a little of the 'real him'." He went up in Obi's estimation.

Monique relates the story of how she got her mother to the hospital. The day had started badly. Someone damaged the wall near Dame Marguerite's gate and her mother was also worried about other personal matters. Monique was at her business at Lyford Cay.

> It was around three o'clock, quarter to three, Verla, the housekeeper called: "Your mummy sick." "What happen?" "Gas ... she's crying in pain, she got it bad, bad, you come." I closed down the shop ... Mummy nags Leslie and me to death if something is seriously wrong ... so I was between two minds but said to myself, you'll never live this down. I got to Lynmar [the Pindling home] from Lyford Cay in ten minutes. I dashed upstairs and there in the room, Mummy was lying there, "My stomach!" [Leslie interrupts, "She never complained, that's the problem."] "What is it, Mummy?" "It hurts, it hurts!" I touched her stomach and she screamed. I realized something was wrong but I didn't know what to do. We were far from the hospital and at 3:15 p.m. on a Thursday afternoon school is out. How was I going to ... I needed an outrider to get from there to the hospital. So I called the Cable Beach Police Station: "Is Larry Ferguson there? Listen, my mother is ill, we live in the West and I need to get to Princess Margaret Hospital. There's too much traffic. Could you send an outrider to me?" "Who's this?" I realized I didn't identify myself. "This is Monique Pindling and my mother, Lady Pindling, is ill." The police replied, "We will be there in five minutes. Just hold on."

> We changed Mummy's clothes and by the time we got her dressed, I could hear the siren coming down the road ... I dashed downstairs, got the car out of the garage, opened the gate. The motorcyclist came up the road ... got Mummy in the car.

> The outrider asked where were we going. I answered, Princess Margaret Hospital. He said: "Listen to me, stay close to me. When you see my hand, do like this. You do as I tell you and don't fall far from me." [I said] "Mummy, sit in the car and hold on."

> We got out of the gate, got to Prospect Ridge traffic light. I couldn't reach anyone. Couldn't get Leslie's cell phone, called Obi, couldn't get him; called Michelle, couldn't get nobody.

I was only able to reach Sandy [Michelle's husband] and told him I was taking her mother to the Princess Margaret Hospital and asked him to call Michelle, Leslie and Obi, and tell them to "get to the hospital now as I don't know what to do, bye". Then I only had two seconds before the traffic light changed. I called Danny [Monique's husband] and asked him to call the hospital to tell them I was on the way with my mummy in the back seat: "She has a terrible pain in her stomach and is vomiting and she feels ill."

I couldn't talk anymore, as the outrider said "Let's go", and from the time we left that light, we drove down the middle of the road and I was going 50 miles per hour, lights on; Mummy in the back seat – "Nicki! Nicki!" – every bump, she felt her stomach hurt. We drove down the middle of the road, of West Bay Street, Bay Street. We got to emergency and pulled right up to the door; Danny had everyone outside. When I opened the door, the nurses came out, Mummy vomited. They took her out of the car, put her in the wheelchair and took her into the examination room. I stood there pacing up and down: where are these brothers and sister that I have? I was alone. The nurses had to register her.... You had to put her mother's name and date of birth. They asked for next of kin. I said "Me, I'm the only one here." "No, you have to put the mother's name." "But her mother's dead!" They asked other questions which I could not answer. By that time, Michelle arrived. Then Obi. Leslie went to the house to pack clothes in case she had to stay overnight.

Obi was on his way to St Andrew's School with his second son, Andrew, to coach QC's softball team in a game against St Andrew's when he got a call from a police officer who said: "Obi, your sister just called here; she's in a panic; she just took your mother to the hospital; they had to get there with an outrider; you better get there."

Sandy finally got through to Michelle – she was in a meeting and Sandy told her to go to the hospital immediately.

Monique had had a similar experience when she took her father to the hospital during his illness. She said to her mother afterwards: "If you were not a Pindling you would be dead because there was no way they would send an outrider, and an ambulance would have had difficulty getting to us."

The first diagnosis was that Dame Marguerite had a gastro-intestinal problem and could be released in an hour; but Dr Duane Sands, after examining her, told them it was serious – very, very bad. "It's touch and go."

She had tests, and within two hours she had pneumonia; in three hours her kidneys shut down. She had gone from okay to critical. She had shortness of breath and the doctors had to put two holes in her side, one to pump out the blood from the stomach and one to drain the liquid out of the lungs. She needed two tubes, one for air and one for food in the form of liquid protein. She was jaundiced a little and in order for them to see if her body would naturally emit the fluids, they pumped her full of fluids ... but they had to insert more tubes to get rid of the fluid. She was extremely ill. Dr Sands admitted: "The next 72 hours are critical." Monique says she was numb.

Dame Marguerite spent ten days in the intensive care unit and then another ten on the private surgical ward. When she was progressing well, staff walked her over to the physiotherapy room, and put her on the treadmill. Leslie says when he saw her, he thought he was going to die. He was laughing. She was giggling herself. The nurses asked Leslie to bring some shorts for his Mother. Dame Marguerite very quickly stated: "I do not wear shorts."

Leslie and Monique say that it was frightening and strange not to have her in the house, which "echoed with silence". "Mummy was the glue that held us together and it was odd not having her there." The children also missed having lunch with her.

Leslie and Monique say that their mother relies more on them "for the running of her day to day life; she still thinks of Michelle as 'the legal political mind of our family' but says that 'we are a very strong family'." The nurses commented, 'You all close, eh? You come to your mummy some time once, twice, three times a day. Every day.' I said, 'What you mean?' 'Well some people don't see their families for days.' She said a patient had twelve children and none came to see her." Monique adds that she was upset that she could only stay ten to fifteen minutes a visit. For the first couple of days in hospital, Monique and Leslie admit that their mother did not open her eyes – for 48 hours her eyes were closed, and Monique panicked. But there were days when she really was alert, she could have a conversation. Monique never witnessed this as most of the time when she visited, her mother was resting; she bathed her or changed her bed pan, and one day she cried and said, "I never get to say anything." So one day Michelle and her friends got together and told Monique she needed a break. "I don't know how this nurse found me ... she called me – said she knew I was upset because I never got to speak to her. I was so happy when my mother said 'Nicki, the nurse said you were so upset that you didn't get to talk to me today'. I said 'Yes mummy, your eyes were closed or you were resting' ... Everyone started to cry." After her discharge from hospital she made a complete recovery and was able to continue her usual activities.

Dame Marguerite does not remember how ill she was. The children surmise that she was worried about all of them – not only them, but about Perry Christie (the former Prime Minister), about Hubert Ingraham (the Prime Minister), The Bahamas (period), the children, the crime, education. Leslie says that he feels that with our leadership today, people don't care as much. Monique adds that sometimes she thinks their mother sees her life's work going down the drain; that it hurts her when she sees all this crime and wonders what the people of The Bahamas are going to do. But Leslie tries to reassure her that they've come a long way:

> *I don't think I've ever seen more proud black people in my life and not only that, you can go Over the Hill to that clapboard house and you can go to the Red Cross Ball and the same man and woman who live in that house dress right up. Bahamians don't feel limited by anything. They can go anywhere. When you travel abroad and people look at you differently and then you mention that you are from The Bahamas, their whole attitude changes. Therefore that's a proud thing for my parents to know and realize.*

Leslie and Monique agree that their mother did not know her strength until she became ill. They, like Michelle, were amazed at the reaction of everyone, PLP, FNM, Black, White, Yellow – all were concerned and asked about her progress. She is revered throughout the country and still given courtesies although she is not an official part of government.

Dame Marguerite's career culminated when she received the high honour of Dame Commander of the Most Distinguished Order of Saint Michael and Saint George from Her Majesty Queen Elizabeth II in 2007. Michelle relates how proud she felt at the investiture and how elegant and poised her mother was at the ceremony.

As she said herself at a luncheon afterwards, "Who would have thought that someone from Long Bay Cays in Andros with the background she had … to think that she rose to that level, that stature. I was really, really proud."

Epilogue

Marguerite McKenzie Pindling, a woman from humble beginnings, stood loyally at the side of her husband, Lynden Oscar Pindling, during his long career as lawyer, Leader of the Opposition, Premier and Prime Minister. She raised a wonderful family but also played an important role as First (political) Lady; later in her own right she was appointed deputy to the Governor-General and received a damehood for services to The Bahamas.

It is quite extraordinary that Marguerite Pindling, with a limited formal education, was able to grasp the intricacies of politics so quickly. In her capacity as wife of the Leader of the Opposition, Premier and Prime Minister, she was able to influence public policy through her intuitiveness, shrewdness, dogged determination and tenacity. Indeed, Sir Arthur Foulkes, who served in an early Pindling Cabinet, states that Dame Marguerite played a significant role in influencing the history of The Bahamas.

He cites an example from 1967, when Lynden Pindling was reluctant to change his safe constituency in Grant's Town for the risky one in Andros. Cyril Stevenson was very popular there. But, as Sir Arthur recalls, "Lady Pindling convinced her husband to run in Andros, her birthplace, after being lobbied by members of the party. In fact she thought the switch of constituencies was a brilliant idea." Lynden Pindling's popularity and his colour were perhaps the only means by which the PLP could defeat Cyril Stevenson. Sir Arthur believes that had Lynden Pindling not run in Andros, the PLP would have been one seat down and the United Bahamian Party (UBP) would have won in 1967.

Another example of Dame Marguerite's political savvy, cited by Sir Arthur Foulkes, occurred in 1963, when some PLP party members tried to force Lynden Pindling to step down. Lady Pindling had the presence of mind to call *The Bahamian Times* office, where members of the National Committee for Positive Action (NCPA), the radical wing of the party, were working. She was convinced that members of the NCPA would support her husband as the best man to lead the PLP. Arthur Foulkes was present but was preparing the paper for publication, so Jeffrey Thompson agreed to go to the Pindling home. Thompson ensured that Lynden Pindling remained as leader and the attempted "Christmas coup" failed. Again, Marguerite Pindling saved the day. This incident was a crucial turning point in the history of the party (the PLP) and The Bahamas.

Monique and Leslie Pindling think that their mother was more political than their father. They describe her as a "go-get-it-done politician", an attitude which took a lot of strength and energy, as did her efforts to unite everyone. Often Sir Lynden would ask her to deal with certain problems while he was busy with other matters. She enjoyed such undertakings. Lady Pindling knew everybody; so much so that the fellows around her husband "did not mess with Marguerite", as "to get to him, you had to go through her ... she was a fighter and could hold her own ... she will always be revered ... she played a significant role."

As a political figure, she made some mistakes and was open to much criticism. Many unkind things were said about her and her husband. But inner strength enabled her to weather the storm. Her sense of duty and service to Sir Lynden and the nation is unquestionable. Soon after recovering from her serious illness in 2007, she continued attending national functions, and was eager to revitalize the Lynden Pindling Memorial activities and to continue her work in charitable organizations.

A lady of style, Dame Marguerite always takes care of her physical appearance. Her beauty and dress sense have won international attention. When attending Commonwealth Heads of Government Meetings (CHOGM) abroad, she always ended up on the front page of some newspaper, impeccably dressed. She is stunning whatever the function and even when wearing very casual clothes. She has had a great impact on fashion, and Bahamian women admit that her stylishness caused them to pay closer attention to their own appearance.

Dame Marguerite's children are proud of her and their late father. As Michelle states: "As proud as we are of our parents, they are of us." The Pindlings are a close-knit family and love abounds. Dame Marguerite is as protective of her children as she was of her late husband, Sir Lynden Pindling, whose charisma is legend.

Personally, I have found Dame Marguerite to be a sincere and loyal friend. During the high and low points in my life, she has always been there for me and my late husband, Winston Saunders, who had a special relationship with her. Her visit to me in hospital in 1992 after surgery was an unforgettable occasion. I was gratified by her presence when I received an honorary doctorate from the University of the West Indies at Mona, Jamaica, in 2005. Not only was she present, she hosted a dinner for me, my family and a few friends. After the sudden death of my husband, in Jamaica in November 2006 she was at the airport to meet me, despite the late hour. She always looked out for Winston and me at various national functions and we sometimes travelled to the Family Islands with her and the family.

Her deep sense of duty drove Dame Marguerite to serve her country and the Bahamian people for over 50 years. Despite her public life, she was able to maintain a household, raise four children and support her husband. Naturally, she was more sympathetic towards PLPs, but had many acquaintances who were not party members or supporters. She has few regrets except perhaps for the few times she did or said something that embarrassed her husband.

She states:

> *When I look back over my life and I think things over, I can truly say that I've been blessed and I give thanks to God for what he has done for me – this little Island girl. And I thank Pindling for exposing me to that particular kind of life, and it was no ordinary life – to meet world leaders and their ladies and to sit at the feet of some of them …*

Yes, she has lived and is still living an extraordinary life!

Notes

CHAPTER 1
1. Michael Craton, *Pindling: The Life and Times of Lynden Oscar Pindling (1930–2000), First Prime Minister of The Bahamas* (Macmillan Caribbean, 2002), 61.
2. Gail Saunders, *Bahamian Society after Emancipation* (Ian Randle Publishers, Kingston, 2003), 60.
3. Ibid. 90.

CHAPTER 4
1. Felicia R. Lee, "Bahamians Fear, Revere First Lady", *The Miami Herald*, Monday 8 June 1987.

CHAPTER 5
1. Interview with Lady Pindling, 23 September 2003.
2. Ibid.
3. Saunders, *Bahamian Society after Emancipation*, 151–2.
4. Paul Albury, *The Story of The Bahamas* (Macmillan Caribbean, London, 1975), 212.
5. Ibid.
6. Gail Saunders, "Social History of The Bahamas, 1890–1953", Ph.D dissertation (University of Waterloo, Ontario, Canada), 409; Michael Bloch, *The Duke of Windsor's War* (London, 1982).
7. Saunders, "Social History", 415.
8. *Nassau Magazine*, 1 January 1942, vol. ix, no. 2, p. 8.
9. Saunders, "Social History", 415–16.
10. *The Bahamas Handbook Businessmen's Annual*, 1978/1979 (Dupuch Publications, Nassau, 1979), 89.
11. Opening Remarks by Lady Pindling at the 1984 Red Cross Fair, Clarence Town, Long Island, Friday 30 March 1984.
12. Interview with Lady Pindling, 23 September 2003.
13. *Nassau Guardian*, 22 January 1986.
14. Tribute to Lady Marguerite Pindling, Red Cross Ball, 24 January 2005.

CHAPTER 6
1. Gail Saunders, "The Making of a Leader: The Ascendancy of Lynden Oscar Pindling as Leader of the Progressive Liberal Party, 1953–1963", in Brian Moore and Swithin Wilmot (eds.), *Before and After 1865: Education, Politics and Regionalism in the Caribbean* (Ian Randle Publishers, Kingston, 1998), 172.
2. Ibid. See also Hartley Saunders, *The Other Bahamas* (Nassau, 1991), 341–3.
3. Saunders, "The Making of a Leader", 172.
4. Craton, *Pindling*, 389.
5. Colin Hughes, *Race and Politics in The Bahamas* (University of Queensland Press, St Lucia (Queensland) and London, 1981), 103–4.
6. Ibid. 104.
7. *Nassau Guardian*, 26 June 1964. See also Hughes, *Race and Politics in The Bahamas*, 104.
8. Ibid. 160.
9. Ibid.

10. *Nassau Guardian*, 10 May 1987.
11. Interview with A. Leonard Archer, 18 June 2008.
12. *Nassau Guardian*, 20 June 1983.
13. Ibid.
14. Ibid.
15. Andrew Coakley, *Nassau Guardian*, "Bahamians owe me, declares Lindy Pindling", 3 June 1987.
16. Ibid.
17. *Nassau Guardian*, 10 June 1987.
18. Ibid.
19. *The Tribune*, 9 June 1987.
20. Basil Smith, *Bahamian Review Magazine*, August 1987, 13.
21. Ibid.

CHAPTER 7
1. Michael Craton and Gail Saunders, *Islanders in The Stream: A History of The Bahamian People*, vol. ii (The University of Georgia Press, Athens and London, 1998), 375.
2. Ibid. 376.
3. Craton, *Pindling*, 300.
4. Craton and Saunders, *Islanders in The Stream*, ii. 377–8.
5. Gail Saunders, Foreword in Olga C. Jenkins, *Bahamian Memories: Island Voices of the Twentieth Century* (University Press of Florida, Gainesville, 2000), p. xvii.
6. Craton, *Pindling*, 304. From an interview with Sir Lynden Pindling, 17 December 1998.
7. Ibid.
8. Craton and Saunders, *Islanders in The Stream*, ii. 382.
9. Lee, "Bahamians Fear, Revere First Lady".
10. Craton and Saunders, *Islanders in The Stream,* ii. 382.
11. Craton, *Pindling*, 310.

CHAPTER 8
1. Craton, Pindling, 38.
2. Ibid. 284.
3. Ibid. 316.
4. Ibid. 319.
5. Ibid. 317.
6. Ibid. 419.
7. Ibid. 288.

CHAPTER 9
1. Craton, Pindling, 389.
2. Ibid. 377
3. Ibid. 383
4. Ibid. 389; Patricia Beardsley Roker (ed.), *The Vision of Sir Lynden Pindling in His Own Words* (Nassau, 2001), 166–74.

Index

addresses. *see* speeches
ambassador for The
   Bahamas, MP as,
   34–5
Andros, childhood on, 1–11
Archer, A. Leonard, 61–2

Beaux Arts Ball, 37–8
Black Tuesday, 23–6
Boyd, Lennox, 20
Brayen, Alvin R., 28
Butler, Milo, 22–3

campaigning
  extent of, 55
  Kemp's Bay, 26–8
  South Andros, 27–8
Cat Island Women,
   gaoling of, 57–8
charity work, 35–6, 94–5.
   see also Red Cross
Charles, Prince of Wales,
   32
childhood, 1–7
children, 19, 20
  closeness with parents,
    102–4
  on legacy of parents, 107
  on MP as politician,
    104–5, 108, 117
  on MP's pancreatitis,
    110–14
  on MP's style and
    elegance, 108–10
  MP's support of during
    illness, 107–8
  not treated as different,
    99–102
  realisation of parents'
    importance, 99
  strict upbringing, 98–9
Christmas in Andros, 7–8
church attendance, 8–9,
   36–7
clothes, 13, 31–4, 117
Commonwealth Heads of
   Government Meetings
  Bahamas 1985, 78–80
  first, 75–6

Jamaica 1975, 76–7
  London 1977, 77–8
  Zimbabwe 1991, 80
concerts in Andros, 8
constitution, new, of
   1963, 21
coronation of Queen
   Elizabeth II, 75
corruption accusations
   against Lynden
   Pindling, 69–74, 105
courtship by Lynden
   Pindling, 14–15

Dale Carnegie Course,
   19–20
DCMG honours, 95
death, rituals concerning
   in Andros, 8
driving test, 18
drug trafficking
  corruption accusations
    against Lynden
    Pindling, 69–74
  through the Bahamas,
    68–9

education, 6–7, 12, 19
elections
  1956, 17–18
  1960, 20
  1962, 21
  1967, 28–9
  PLP defeat in Aug
    1992, 83–4
  PLP defeat in March
    1997, 88
Elizabeth II, Queen, 43,
   75, 76
Empire Day in Andros, 8
employment, 12–13, 17,
   18–19
entertaining, 30–1

family life, 30
father, 1, 2, 3
Fawkes, Randol, 28
Fountain, Patricia (Patsy),
   19

Free National Movement,
   66, 78
fundraising for the PLP,
   18. *see also* charity
   work

General Strike 1958, 20
Guildhall, London, speech
   at, 34–5

hats, 33
honeymoon, 16

Isaacs, Lady Patricia, 19

James, Erica, 33
Johnson, Doris, 12, 20
Johnson, Livingstone B.,
   15–16

Kemp's Bay, campaigning
   in, 26–7

Lightbourn, Helena,
   12–13
Loyalist Memorial
   Sculpture Garden, 38
loyalty to husband, 30

Mail Boat in Andros, 7
majority rule, 28
Mandela, Nelson, 80
Manuel, Gladys, 39–40
marriage to Lynden
   Pindling, 15–16
McKenzie, Bertie (half-
   brother), 9
McKenzie, Reuben Daniel
   (father), 2, 3, 11,
   19–11
McKenzie, Viola "Mirmie"
   Duncombe (mother),
   1, 5–6

Nassau, life as single
   woman in, 12–14
National Committee
   for Positive Action
   (NCPA), 21

pancreatitis, 96–7,
  110–14
patron of the arts, MP as,
  37–8
Pindling, Leslie (son), 19.
  see also children
Pindling, Lynden
  asks wife for opinion,
    60
  Black Tuesday
    demonstrations,
    23–6
  cancer diagnosis, 88, 89
  CHOGM in the
    Bahamas 1985,
    79–80
  at coronation of Queen
    Elizabeth II, 75
  corruption accusations
    against, 69–74, 105
  courtship by, 14–15
  death, 90–2
  and dismantling of
    apartheid, 79–80
  early work for MP with,
    17, 18–19
  elected as Parliamentary
    Leader, 17–18
  elected Chairman of
    PLP, 21
  knighthood, 80–2
  loyalty to, MP's, 55–7
  marriage to, 15–16
  memorial lecture series,
    93–4
  resignation in 1997, 88
  Sir Lynden Pindling
    Foundation, 92–3
  stays as leader after
    1992 defeat, 84–5
  tribute to wife, 88
Pindling, Marguerite. *see
  also* speeches
  childhood, 1–7
  children, 19, 20
  criticisms of, way of
    facing, 58–9
  DCMG honours, 95,
    115
  as Deputy to the
    Governor General,
    95–6

driving test, 18
impact of PLP's 1967
  victory, 29
intolerance of disloyalty,
  59
life in opposition after
  1992, 85–8
pancreatitis, 96–7,
  110–14
political savvy of,
  116–17
role in keeping husband
  in power, 58
rumours of standing for
  election, 60
Sir Lynden's tribute
  to, 88
social life after 2007
  defeat, 96
tribute to at Red Cross
  Annual Ball 2005,
  52–4
Pindling, Monique. *see*
  children
Pindling, Obafemi (son),
  19, 104–5. *see also*
  children
Pindling-Sands, Michelle
  (daughter), 20, 92–3,
  94, 107–8. *see also*
  children
Platas, Rosa, 32
prayer breakfasts, 93
Progressive Liberal Party
  (PLP), 18, 20–1, 22–3

Red Cross
  establishment in
    Bahamas, 43
  national fairs in the
    Family Islands, 46–8
  national status in 1973,
    46
  new headquarters, 48–9
  opening of new
    headquarters,
    49–52
  services provided, 48
  start of MP's
    involvement, 46
  tribute to MP at Annual
    Ball 2005, 52–4

during WWII in the
  Bahamas, 44–5
Rutherford, Cynthia, 31–2

Second World War,
  Bahamas during, 43–4
Sir Lynden Pindling
  Foundation, 92–3
Smith, Basil, 66
South Andros,
  campaigning in, 27–8
speeches
  controversial, during
    June 1987
    campaign, 65–7
  first Women's
    Convention of the
    PLP, 62–3
  Guildhall in London,
    34–5
  Mothers' Club, May
    1982, 40–2
  new headquarters for
    Red Cross, 49–52
  at schools in Andros,
    38–9
  Women's Regional
    Branches of the
    PLP, 60–2
Symonette, Sir Roland
  and Lady Margaret,
  31

Thompson, Merlene, 59

United Bahamian Party,
  20–1

votes for women, 20

Wallace-Whitfield, Cecil,
  59–60
wedding of Prince Charles
  and Lady Diana, 82
women
  encouragement of by
    MP, 39–40
  MP on contribution
    of, 60–2
  running for office,
    MP's opinion on, 40–2
  votes for, 20